PRAISE for *Not With*

Juanita's book makes education activism seem possible for anyone who cares enough to do it at any level . . . baking cookies, making posters and buttons, or running for public office. It's a good balance of warnings about the potholes of activism and how-to encouragement.

—Teresa Saum
Coordinator of the Minnesota Coalition for Authentic Reform in Education

"No child left behind," they say? Just where do they think they're taking my child? "It's time for parents, teachers and local community members everywhere to gang up and take back our schools," writes Juanita Doyon. In this invaluable guidebook for the would-be activist, Juanita distills the best from her many years of education activism and delightfully details how to maximize your effectiveness in this noble endeavor!

—Tom Jasper
Parent and elementary school teacher in the Pacific Northwest for 35 years

Ever wish you knew a fellow activist whom you could consult any time, day or night, and know that she (or he) would bring a balance of informed authority, shared concern, and a terrific sense of humor to bear? Reading this book is like having an experienced rabble-rouser (I can think of no higher compliment) at your side to cheer you on with both practical and philosophical bits of wisdom. Juanita practically brings you milk and cookies! What a treat!

I can tell that this is the sort of book I'll want to keep handy on my shelf for the occasional shot in the arm, or a jog of my memory. On behalf of many parents who weren't sure there was anything they could do to make a difference, "Thank you, Room Mother for the Resistance!"

—Marcia Weinert
Home schooling mother and educational activist
Coordinator, "Putting Children First," Webster, New York

Every community needs Juanita Doyon. Quick with a quip, Juanita brings common sense and practical cynicism to the task of empowering parents and teachers. Each chapter is full of sane, practical, and sometimes wildly funny examples of how real people can change the world.

Juanita's brand of cheerful activism is democracy at its most profound and most practical levels.

As a parent of four children, Juanita knows there is no such thing as a standard child. She respects those—mostly parents and teachers—who really know children up close and personally. In this book she shares simple strategies for finding and joining with others to defeat corporate-driven standards and accountability schemes.

To the suits in administrative offices in state capitals, who scream "Accountability!" at teachers and parents, Juanita replies "Suits, account for thyselves!"

—George Sheridan
President, Black Oak Mine Teachers Association, CTA/NEA
Garden Valley, California

NOT WITH OUR KIDS YOU DON'T!

Ten Strategies to Save Our Schools

Juanita Doyon

HEINEMANN ■ Portsmouth, NH

Heinemann
A division of Reed Elsevier Inc.
361 Hanover Street
Portsmouth, NH 03801-3912
www.heinemann.com

Offices and agents throughout the world

© 2003 by Juanita Doyon

Library of Congress Cataloging-in-Publication Data
Doyon, Juanita.
Not with our kids you don't! : ten strategies to save our schools /
Juanita Doyon.
p. cm.
Includes bibliographical references.
ISBN 0-325-00486-2
1. Educational change—United States. 2. Education—Parent
participation—United States. I. Title.
LA217.2 .D694 2003
371. 1'00973—dc21   2002013704

Editor: Lois Bridges
Production service: bookworks
Production coordinator: Elizabeth Valway
Cover design: Linda Knowles
Typesetter: Technologies 'N Typography
Manufacturing: Steve Bernier
Back cover photo by Charlie Davis

Printed in the United States of America on acid-free paper
07 06 05 04 03 DA 1 2 3 4 5

To my Dad, who taught me to dazzle them with my footwork.

The significant problems we face cannot be solved at the same level of thinking we were at when we created them.

—Albert Einstein

*C*ontents

oreword

I am pleased to introduce readers to Juanita Doyon. I met her wit and pomposity-bursting voice first in e-mail and then in person when she drove two hours to pick me up at the Seattle Airport. Gadfly, expert, button queen, candidate for Superintendent of Public Instruction, Juanita writes letters to the editor, appears on TV interviews, stands on street corners handing out anti-testing literature, and keeps up voluminous e-mail correspondence with students, superintendents, teachers, professors, and parents across the country. Oh, and in her spare time, she designed and stamped out 25,000 test resistance buttons in the past year.

Whether it's a superintendent of schools in New York, a mom in Texas, a professor in Massachusetts, or a high schooler in Colorado, when Juanita hears about a resister, she sends buttons.

Juanita's own children will be safely out of high school before the penalties of her state's high-stakes exit exam kick in, and class party cupcakes and band fundraising are behind her. But this doesn't mean the indefatigable kid-supporter is going to take a rest. As a passionate advocate for public schools and for all the children in them, Juanita is out pounding the pavement for all the kids whose lives are threatened by high-stakes tests.

Juanita was ahead of the pack in recognizing how the federal government is usurping local control of schools through the *No Child Left Behind* legislation. While the rest of us were dozing, Juanita carried her press card from *Substance*, the Chicago-based newspaper of the resistance, into the halls of conferences touting this legislation before the bill even passed Congress. In Reno, Juanita teamed up with Professor Michelle Trusty-Murphy to work the conference halls. Noting that the session presenters expected educators and parents to kneel at the data altar, Juanita concludes, "We came; we saw; we felt sick to our stomachs."

Next, Juanita heard that some moms in Texas were thinking of traveling to San Antonio to picket the *No Child Left Behind* conference, so she jumped on a plane and joined them. As Texas mom and organizer Carol Holst observes, "If actions speak louder than words, then our soft-spoken Juanita issues volumes. She flew all the way to San Antonio to help us crash the *No Child Left Behind* conference. And she did it out of the goodness of her heart."

The Texas moms had planned to picket the conference, but when they spotted a spare table in the exhibit area, they regarded it as "a sign," and immediately set up shop—right alongside the people selling materials to support the government initiative. "It was so very nice of the Department of Education to provide a booth for us," says this roving room mother of the resistance.

The moms talked to everybody who paused—passing out buttons and stickers. Before half the day was over, people who had spotted the buttons being worn came searching out the table of contraband. Juanita notes, "There was no resistance to our resistance. People came up and said we were the best thing about the conference."

Juanita's buttons were also hot items at appearances she made in Rochester, New York and Baltimore, Maryland. Juanita calls these jaunts "button delivery/networking sessions." She's happy to meet e-mail buddies from the FairTest discussion list, and when she meets parents and educators worried about the tests, she recruits them to become resisters. Back home in Washington, she leaves buttons in restaurants, restrooms, on store counters, and any other place she thinks a parent or educator might pick one up. Not a bad strategy for an organizer whose motto is "One resister at a time." Recently asked if she'd speak at a college if an organizer could round up ten people, Juanita replied, "I'll come if there are two people who will listen—and take a button."

Behind every button there's a story. Juanita can tell you about the 8th grader who received a supply last year and is now back, asking for 50 more—so he can educate this year's 7th graders about test resistance. Juanita reminds these kids to ask their parents, to be polite, to become informed about the issues, and to reach out to others. She is building responsible citizenship in a way no test can.

Bill Cala, superintendent of schools in New York told Juanita about two high school students who were interested in test resistance. Within hours, Juanita was communicating with the students, getting them to work on button designs and strategies for high stakes test resistance. Bill says, "I don't think you can find a more giving, dedicated, caring and sincere person." He adds, "She's the real deal."

That's what Juanita offers in this book: the real deal. She offers the experiences and inspirations of a mom who is out to save public education. Readers will soon discover that Juanita does not suffer political doubletalk lightly. As she asks early in the book, "No child left behind where?" No child vomiting on a test? No child labeled for life? As a mom who cares about kids, Juanita reminds everybody that children are where the focus must be—not standards, not tests, not reading methods—but children. And, as anyone who has more than one child knows, children are different. Different kids need different approaches and materials. One size definitely does not fit all.

If Juanita doesn't trust politicians, she does trust her children's teachers. "To date, I figure my kids have experienced the teaching of 90 great teachers, and, as everything from popcorn chairperson to site council chair, I have worked with many more." She wants her children's teachers to decide pass or fail, not a $10-an-hour temp worker. Juanita argues that a student who has jumped through the hoops of some 50 certified teachers for 13 years should not be blocked from the certificate of the rite of passage by one test written by a testing company. Juanita urges parents to opt their children out of the tests in elementary school. "Any child who takes the test is encouraging the state to continue down the wrong path."

Poking fun at the jargon of the standards-and-testing spin meisters, Juanita says, "They want 'world class?' We're going to give them a 'world class' fight!"

"We are the gabby moms and dads," announces Juanita with a smile. "I'm just a parent, and I can say anything." Then she adds, "And what I'm saying right now is that 'We won't WASL.'" Founder of Mothers Against WASL (the Washington State test), Juanita plans to become the state Superintendent of Public Instruction in 2004.

You are about to read the words of a mom who believes pas-
sionately that one person can make a difference. Of course, she will
say with a smile, two working together make an even bigger difference. Enter these pages and join Juanita in the fight to support public education.

Susan Ohanian

*Susan Ohanian, a longtime teacher, maintains a website on the politics of
education (www.susanohanian.org) and is a Senior Fellow at the Vermont Society for the Study of Education.*

An Activist by Any Other Name

Broaching the topic of activism with those involved in education, I discovered that many who I consider my closest allies or fellow activists don't categorize themselves as activists whatsoever. This left me with a dilemma—and no audience for this book. Good grief! Now, what?

An effective strategy used often by the hierarchy is to redefine words, not to mention educational theory, for their own purposes. For the novice parent or concerned citizen, accepted definitions can even be found on governmental and nonprofit education websites. So, I think it only fair that I borrow this strategy, for a moment, and redefine a word of my own. For the purpose of this book and encouragement of all who struggle to eke out their own educational sanity:

ac·tiv·ist, *n.* one who is not satisfied with the status quo, is frustrated, angered, or disgusted by events taking place, or sees injustice in the activities or policies of others; one who speaks of this dissatisfaction to others and encourages action; one who communicates with others, presenting information or opinion that can be used to bring about change in an undesirable situation; one whose occupation creates change and improvement; one who questions authority in any way; one who bucks the system or helps others to do so; those who act on their own convictions; brave souls fighting, in some small or large way, for what they believe is right.

Accelerated Agitation

Used to be, I was just-a-parent in a big sea of parents attending open house or the group of three parents attending PTA meetings at my local school: baking cute little trays of cupcakes for classroom parties and chaperoning field trips to the zoo or science center. I was content and happy in my public education world of twenty-seven-kid classrooms and Friday take-home progress reports. I even went where not many parents had gone before and delivered home-baked goodies of appreciation to the teachers' lounge on occasion. I admired those mothers who seemed to live at school, so I became one of them.

Then one day I got angry about a decision that was made to re-locate our elementary school's kindergarten program. Those in charge were not listening to reason. I made a presentation to the school board. I felt good about it. My first attempt to find educa-tional justice made little difference at the time, but, suddenly, I was a known advocate for children, schools, parents, and teachers, in my own school and in the school district. I was no longer satisfied baking cupcakes, planning Valentine parties, and writing an occa-sional letter to the editor to support school funding proposals, though I did continue these vital cocurricular activities to my new-found call to activism.

As it happens, my four children span the most recent age of ed-ucation reform. My oldest daughter, Doris, began kindergarten in 1985, two years after the education department report *A Nation at Risk* declared war on the status quo of American public schools. Using inflammatory—jump on the bandwagon or continue walking the road to education-hell—propaganda, *A Nation at Risk* detailed widespread failure in our public schools. With little regard for vari-ations in exterior circumstance, this report began blanket reforms of the system, which have culminated in today's standards and testing for all.

Through my children's education, I have witnessed and fought against a deterioration of communication and an increase of pressure on parents, students, teachers, and local administration to conform and perform. I have observed an increasing disregard at the state and national level for the needs in classrooms and communities. Serving on a school site council—a group of parents, community members, and school personnel working to direct school improvement—over the past ten years, I have experienced frustration as our charge has been narrowed from self-study and council-chosen improvement goals, which included parental involvement, school climate, technology, safety, and academics, to state- and district-mandated goals of math and reading test score improvement.

My children continue to experience high-quality education, because we are fortunate to have good teachers and capable local administrators, but I fear that by the time my youngest children are in high school, curriculum and teaching will be totally devoted to test preparation for our state's Washington Assessment of Student Learning (WASL). In fact, this is the stated goal of Washington's education leaders, who boldly broadcast the message: "If teachers teach to the WASL they are teaching what students need for the 21st century."

Public education is in trouble, and it needs me. It needs you too, needs you to step beyond your typical role as teacher or parent or administrator. If you are eager to become an effective educational activist, with the most bang for your time and your buck, then you've picked up the right book. If you simply want to be able to find educational sanity for your own child in public school, help is here. If you are struggling to balance devotion to the school system and government that pays you and your need to live with the job you do for kids, read on.

Each of us involved in education has a point at which inappropriate or unfair policies collide with our conscience or our good sense. For parents, the call to activism can be the forty-pound backpack destroying our fourth grader's posture or district-mandated sock color for our eighth grader. For teachers it can be the district crabbing about our students' test scores and requiring us to attend expensive yet worthless "professional development," while we're assigned thirty-four students per period, in an unheated portable with mold-infested walls. For administrators it can be idiotic standardized curriculum or a lack of community involvement and support. Any educational concern is a worthy cause for action.

Finding a comfort zone and weighing the time and the risks involved are the only ways to survive as an activist. Not only does education offer equal opportunity for activism, no matter what your age or occupation, it also offers involvement opportunity whether you have an hour or a lifetime to commit. Stick your neck out as far as you like, or work quietly in the background, encouraging the out-there activism of others.

Because most of the local problems in education today stem from decisions made at the state and national level, I have taken my fight for educational justice further than I would have ever imagined. "Think globally; act locally" is not just an environment-friendly, bumper sticker saying anymore. Like it or not, American public education policy has become part of the plan for a global economy. Like it or not, state and national government, arm in arm with BIG BUSINESS, stomp in and act out their best interests in our local schools, from the Redwood Forest to the Gulf Stream Waters to the Cascade Foothills. This plan was made for you and me—and our children! Be afraid! Be very afraid!

Many of the examples found in this book detail my current, state and national fight. However, I cut my activist teeth locally, and these same strategies can be applied to any level of education, from classroom to school board to state education committee to national education secretary.

Lately, my life as an activist has changed dramatically and I find myself surprisingly comfortable being quoted and pictured in articles on the front pages of newspapers throughout a three-state region and interviewing in front of the cameras of four television stations all on the same day. As an explanation to those who might sneer, and a deterrent to those tempted to run me down in the district office or state capitol parking lot, my car sports a license plate frame that reads, "Jesus was a shameless agitator too!" Those of us on the bleeding edge of educational reform and improvement need all the help we can get. With that in mind: My world and welcome to it.

Marked for Change

I like to imagine that there was a time when education was a smaller, friendlier world—and of course in some places it was. In a one-room schoolhouse there was more age-span to cover, but the teacher knew which kids belonged to which parents, and parents didn't have to leave a message after the beep or listen to a prerecorded message in order to voice a complaint or get a homework assignment. A rag to wipe off the slate was recycling. Local control was a teacher hashing it out with the kid or parent.

The change from a one-room schoolhouse to a 3,000-student, multilevel high school with a system of fifteen feeder schools was nothing compared to the changes wreaking havoc in our schools today. Mostly, current changes in education are an attempt to educate an evermore-diverse population and do it in a neat and tidy way that guarantees standard outcome. The term *Outcome-Based Education* was fought fiercely in areas of the country where it was first introduced, so the powers that be have transformed the name and repackaged large parts of the philosophy into Standards-Based Education. States were required by an act of congress—Goals 2000—attached to national education legislation to develop state charts and lists of what children should "know and be able to do." Somehow, these goals have morphed into requirements or "standards," which every child must meet before advancing to the next grade—in some districts and states—or receiving a high school diploma—in most states, now or in the near future.

Those directing school reform are not parents or teachers, though they may have at one time dwelt among us and still call themselves by these titles when it serves their purpose. In an attempt to demonstrate compassion and understanding, they may bring up their own past mistakes, as if they now know better and can demonstrate what current teachers are doing all wrong. "When I was in the classroom, I was just like you, making the mistake of thinking children were learning, when their test scores showed they were not."

This brand of empathy can cause a lot of insecurity and second-guessing on the part of new teachers and frustration and rage on the part of more experienced teachers, who know they are working their butts off and dealing the best they can with the human and material needs of today's students and schools.

In the country of education presidents, education governors, education trusts, partnerships for learning, and accountability commissions, few of whom have a deep background in education—much less child development—standards-based education is king and the standardized test is queen. Hand in hand they rule the education world.

In the name of educational accountability and improvement, new categories of humanity and new activities have been created. We have: *teachers on special assignment, task forces,* and *facilitators.* Lots of planning is done, involving all *stakeholders,* and *shared decision-making* takes place to come to *consensus.* This all sounds very impressive and looks really good on slick pamphlets at national education conferences, but someone in the inner office of ed reform seems to have forgotten that we're dealing with children, not widgets, and teachers, not assembly line workers. But, then, removing the imperfect human equation from education is the goal.

A seamless, *Cradle-to-Grave* system is being implemented: public schools responsible for birth to age five early education, to assure that children are ready to learn in kindergarten through high school, which uses standardized curriculum, to put out standard graduates for a standard workforce, all leading to a planned global economy. Is this really what the American public wants from its public schools? Is this really in our country's best interest? Is this what freedom is about in 21st century America?

We're not paranoid. The education government really is out to get us and/or take over the education of our children. All areas of education, from school lunch menus to math textbooks, have become a target of government and business leaders toying with educational theory and practice. Big brother knows best. Want data? So do they! State and national data bases track test scores, family income, parent education, ethnicity, occupational goals, etc. The majority are financed, one way or another, by your tax dollar and mine. Costly, technological overkill is upon us. Sure, there are good things we can learn from looking at data. But we must be wary of data that is collected that has no business being collected, and being shared with entities that have no business sharing in my child's personal information and abilities.

The more demands of tracking, training, gathering, and reporting that are placed on the classroom teacher, the harder it is for the classroom teacher to find time to communicate with parents. Warm and fuzzy elementary conferences aren't very warm and fuzzy anymore. As teachers are told that child-centered education is a myth and that they must remain completely objective when grading student work and conferencing with parents, we get charts and graphs and rubrics—oh, my!

The more education changes, the less parents are able to recognize what is going on in the school lives of their children. The less communication between teacher and parent, the less apt parents are to become involved in their child's school: Bureaucracy creates apathy. As parents are less involved and teachers have less time to communicate, the directors of the system (government) feel the need to regulate teaching and learning: Apathy demands bureaucracy.

The freakish phrase, "No child left behind," slips from the lips of every politician from the president on down. No child left behind where—on the bus at the end of the day? Let's break the statement down a little and decide whether the government really wants improved education for each and every child in our public schools. Is the policy:

No child vomits on a test? According to company policies, standardized tests on which children vomit are to be placed in a plastic bag and returned to the testing company. Test security is priority number one. Who knows who might go through the trash and retrieve secret test questions from under a second-grader's puke?

No child labeled for life? To increase the pressure on children to achieve at a high level in school, government and school officials now encourage businesses to ask for student transcripts, including test scores, even for part-time jobs while in high school. The list of great inventors, philosophers, even politicians and government officials, who did not shine in their public education record, is long and distinguished. Yet, some of these same officials who moved past their childhood imperfections to reach leadership positions in government and business expect today's children to live with the good, the bad, and the ugly of their school records forever.

No child in an overcrowded classroom because funding policies are flawed? Washington state school construction funding requires a 60 percent voter approval at the local level for construction bonds or levies. The junior high my children attend was built for 750 students. It now serves 1,200 students, as our district had been unable to pass a construction bond for nine years, though the district student count grew by 300 students per year.

In 2001, after eight failures, a bond was passed. My children will be in high school when the new junior high is completed. They will graduate the year the new high school is opened to alleviate overcrowding at that level. School facilities needs throughout the country have reached crises status.

No child is taught by an uncertified teacher or a long-term substitute? Teacher and principal shortage is a real problem throughout the country. From personal experience, serving on hiring committees, teacher and principal candidates are often few and far between, particularly in the fields of math and science. My daughter's eighth-grade math class was taught by a man who was retired and came back because the school could find no one else.

Many schools open their doors each fall with vacancies or underqualified staff. At a news conference in the month of February, a member of the Washington Education Association told of seventy-five teaching vacancies in the Seattle School District. States offering bonuses and enticing salaries often send talent scouts to hiring fairs in other states. At our local education job fair held in the Tacoma Dome stadium, recruiters from California often stand outside, signing teachers to move to their state, before they ever enter the building.

No child pushed out of school or denied opportunity to learn because they might lower the test score average? Birmingham, AL, spring of 2000, 522 "underachieving" students are "administratively withdrawn" involuntarily, just before SAT 9 tests are administered.

Other score-raising tricks of the testing trade include labeling students "special ed," when, without test score quotas, they could get along and thrive in a regular classroom. Special remedial programming and test prep are often offered to or required of students who have the best chance to cross the cut-score finish line. This widely used form of educational triage channels resources so they will make schools look good, whether they are serving every child in the best way or not. When in doubt, manipulate the data—and the children.

No child is overwhelmed by process and policy and becomes disenchanted? Even without high stakes, raising the bar of testing often causes it to fall on the heads of children. My first knowledge of our state's test came when a teacher told me my daughter had been crying over a practice math prompt in third grade. WASL testing annually tells more than 70 percent of Washington's fourth, seventh, and tenth graders that they have failed to meet an arbitrary standard, regardless of grades, effort level, or home situation.

No child misses their graduation because a testing company misgraded their exit exam? Minnesota, class of 2000, dozens of seniors missed their graduation, the culminating reward for thirteen years of hard work, because NCS Pearson, the company who grades their high school exit exam, messed up on the grading. NCS Pearson's answer to the snafu was to offer each student $1,000 toward college attendance. In the case of a set of twins, one twin graduated, while the other was denied the right to wear the cap and gown and walk down the aisle because of a grading error.

Unyielding promotion and graduation policies are the government's answer to school failure. Without addressing why or where some schools fail and to what extent, billions of dollars are spent testing children and implementing a one-size-fits-all curriculum, in every public school in the nation.

Accountability! We must have accountability! Accountability for what and to whom? Are our children accountable to government or is our government accountable to our children? It's time we demand answers and action in response to these questions. This is far from a new or original thought on my part:

> Crucial questions confront America today: Will we provide world leadership or display fatal weakness? Will we succeed or fail in the struggle for survival during the years to come?
>
> The answers, I sincerely believe, depend on whether a shortage of teachers, classrooms, and money—with a consequent lack of high quality education—will prove in the long run to be the undoing of our nation.
>
> *John F. Kennedy,* NEA Journal, *January 1958*

The Education Trust is one of many national, nonprofit groups dedicated to educational improvement. Their website <*www.edtrust .org*> banner shouts proudly that "College Begins in Kindergarten." Perhaps this is why our leaders are pushing for a speed-up of childhood itself and pushing five-year-olds to master first-grade curriculum. Forget about "Zero the Hero" and other friendly learning buddies kids. Enter kindergarten math studies at the "Point of Origin." Can you say, "Burnout by fourth grade"? I knew you could.

Sometimes, it seems as if *The Music Man* has come to town and wants us to discard all proven methodology, beckoning for us to blindly buy in to his think-system propaganda. The media-hyped song and dance suggests that if enough pressure is applied, teachers will teach better, children will learn more, and at younger ages, and we won't have to deal with the messy business of societal inequity. Throw out the rulebook of child development; anything you did in the past was mistaken. You got trouble, my friends. Now I know all you folks are the right kind of parents. I'm going to be perfectly frank. I can deal with the trouble with a wave of my hand. That starts with T, rhymes with best (practice). You need a test! A high-stakes test!

La-de-da and fancy uniforms or *standardized dress* can make for a pretty good show for television blurbs and newspaper articles. But true improvement requires that we all be able to read the music, not just hum the tune by ear—or teach by script.

The desire to rule rather than lead is no respecter of political direction. Democrat, Republican, or Independent, our elected leaders contend that it takes a Business Roundtable <*www.brt.org*>-driven hammer to pound our schools into shape.

Just beneath the level of government officials and business interference is a layer of organizations and associations that has the potential for good or evil, depending on the individuals holding leadership positions. If the people who hold the governmental purse strings demand ideological agreement and support from those who speak for the workforce—unions, professional associations, teaching colleges, etc.—well, we've got real trouble, my friends! On the other hand, if the dues-paying members of these organizations demand loyalty from their leaders, some of the top-down bureaucracy could be overcome.

As individuals within professional organizations and parent groups such as PTA, it's time to question authority and transform ourselves from being a herd to being heard. We must become aware of exactly what our local unions, school boards, and parent organizations are supporting on the local, state, and national levels. We must make ourselves aware of the dangerous levels of coercion and day-trading taking place in the areas of curriculum, standards, and methodology. We must make sure that any deserving resolutions are followed through, not bargained away for the sake of order, or swept aside as unachievable.

As I've become increasingly frustrated by the "we know what's best for you" hierarchy, I've come to realize that parents, community members, and professional educators must learn to work together at least as well as those in the education government. If we don't, we will soon be able to find no trace of the teaching, parenting, or community rights and freedoms that we hold dear. Nobody cares about children like politicians and business CEOs care? Give us a break. Let's begin by taking a look at prospective allies and their importance in the fight for true educational reform and justice.

STRATEGY

View Every Individual as a Potential Ally

One by One Wins the Day

Dedication or addiction to doing the right thing can be a scary, lonely feeling, particularly if you are fighting for something that hasn't quite caught anyone else's attention. In single school or district battles, it is extremely important to weigh the pros and cons of rebellion or attack. Remember, after that heated debate at the school board meeting, or the shouting match with the bossy PTA parent, there is a morning after. "I pledge allegiance to the flag . . ." comes pretty early, and you'll be working with the same kid whose parent you just argued with, or sending your child to school with the same teacher you just reported to the board. A careful tongue saves face. Sounds like a good fortune cookie find, huh?

It would be nice to think that in a country with a government based on individual freedoms and pursuit of happiness a teacher or parent or principal could voice any truthful concern or ask any question and not be chastised or treated differently by those they worked with or for. It would be nice to believe that all those in education are fair, open-minded, and endowed with their share of common sense. But, then, if this beauty were truth, there would be no need for activism in the first place.

In the real world, cold shoulders are often turned to the rebel with a cause, and reprimands get handed out liberally to a teacher taking a stand. We all make choices about what things and people and attitudes we can live with and what we must try to change. *Try* is a very important word here. Activism is often its own reward. Living with ourselves and our convictions is often the only goal we can dare to believe in wholeheartedly.

Once you decide that a situation is unlivable, it's time to troll for potential allies. If you shout into a crowd and all you get back is your own echo, it may be time to fall back and think again. It may be that you're acting in haste or you could just be shouting into the wrong crowd. Finding one person who sees your point or agrees with your stand is an excellent place to start.

If you don't feel comfortable approaching coworkers or friends about your concerns, practice on family members or, better yet, turn tables on the telephone survey person who calls at dinnertime. "Sure, I'll tell you all about my grocery shopping habits, if you tell me what you think about high-stakes testing in our schools." It may take a few tries to get your script down, so that you can quickly explain what you're talking about to a cold contact, but fellow test resisters and I have found that telephone solicitors are often quite willing to share their own opinions of and experiences in our education system. Once you realize that there are others out there who share your concerns, it may be easier to talk to those who will be able to join in your quest for improvement. Choose one or more of the following.

Gabby Moms (and Dads)

"I'm just a parent; I can say anything!" This has been my motto-turned-battle-cry for the entire seventeen years I've been a public school parent. It has kept me from seeking anything but volunteer status. They can put me down, but they'll never shut me up!

The experiences of an involved and caring parent are golden. Insight is our middle name. If we learn to find what our own children need to succeed, we can help to find what all children need. Give us some credit; we'll offer you our expertise and maybe even our outspoken mouths. Our empathy for other parents—even difficult ones—can help in dealing with them. We can make your life easier. We can fight for schools and for children on all sides and in the middle.

Dear Principals and Teachers: Put that company-line garbage where it belongs in the bottom desk drawer next to the confiscated toys and bring it out next summer or when the superintendent visits. Once the playing field is leveled, we may even level with you that our kid isn't the perfect little darling we'd like to believe. When more parents and professional educators become a mutual admiration society, we might just regain control of our schools. It's time for this to happen.

Desperately Seeking Teachers and Administrators

All adults have some contact with public schools, even if it's just to vote *no* on a school levy. It is important that we all project ourselves into the world of today's public school employee. It ain't what it used to be. There is no paddleboard in the closet; there is often no parent at home. Respect is a fleeting concept; nothing is sacred. B-bye Beaver, Hello Bart!

It takes a very special person to enter or remain in the profession of education today. From the coercion of the district honcho who answers to the state, to the whiny parent who swears—literally—that their lying little brat who never turns in a completed assignment deserves a B, not an F, teachers and principals catch it from all sides. Education professionals are on the front line fighting for kids, getting little credit for the daily battles won.

I've found the majority of teachers are quite selfless. They teach because they care about children and enjoy working with them. Unfortunately, the conditions in our society and the structuring of our schools have created teachers who are very needy, and often disenchanted. Teachers need kind words and praise. They need helping hands and cookies. They need respect. They need understanding. They need a summer off. They need a lunch break. They need fewer kids in their class and a few more books. It's the little things that count. The most frequently heard request from teachers is, "I just want to teach!"

These same conditions create principals and district-level administrators who struggle daily just to, as one principal I work with says frequently, "keep the lid on." Any day that doesn't involve a tragedy in one form or another is a good day. If the busses run, the toilets flush, the water isn't contaminated, and the lunches arrive on time, they can get on with the task of education.

Teachers and principals have a good idea of what students and the schools that serve them need to be able to do their best. They usually have a grasp of all the troubles of the educational world, whether they voice this knowledge or keep it to themselves. Ask them and they will tell.

Upper-level Educationists

Two years ago, I answered a letter to the editor in our local paper by contacting its author at Washington State University. From there, a world of networking opportunities unfolded before me. I joined several email discussion groups and found other helpful and curious college professors in these groups.

My general interest in education is based in public schools, where I have gained a solid foundation of knowledge and know-how, working closely with teachers, administrators, and other parents. The background I lack is in the theoretical and the sociological beginnings and growth of public education. So I began conversing with professors of English, mathematics, science, and teacher education. What a wonderful way to fill in the blanks in my own formal education. And I love the autographed collection of college curriculum materials I'm amassing!

When I see something that needs fixing, I want to get to the roots of the problem, so that I can be sure the same problem won't immediately grow back. Most serious activists I have found are self-directed learners. One thing that can keep this self-direction on the right track is help in the form of mentorship.

The professors I've approached online seem to appreciate the authentic drive for knowledge that exists in the brain of an activist. Many professors are activists themselves, so there is a mutual understanding. The activism of upper-level educationists is often manifested in research and scholarly tomes. But this research is ignored by the current education government functionaries who choose to acknowledge only the research that rubber-stamps their own narrow vision. It seems obvious to me that the wisdom of those who have made the study of how children learn their life's work should not be disregarded.

Colleges of education are an excellent place to find support for educational causes, both in the teaching staff and students. Those studying to enter the teaching profession are concerned about the same issues that face the rest of us involved in schools. Our higher education institutions are feeling the pressure to conform to standards, just as our elementary and secondary schools are. Blaming school failure on teaching colleges is becoming quite a popular pastime—none of us involved in education are immune to governmental interference.

Staunch Community Members

We know who they are. We think we know how they think. But do we really? There exists a communication gap between adults who are involved in public schools and those who are uninvolved either because of their age or family status.

Those without direct contact with schools may perceive the youth of today only as the mall culture, loud music, hot car, rude minority—and why not? This is the image portrayed by every broadcast medium they encounter. Schools are judged by the test scores in the paper, the graffiti on the nearest overpass, and whether the clerk at the checkout made the correct change.

There are a whole bunch of people out there who are not directly affected by the length of the school day or the quality of the curriculum or class size or teacher shortage or, or, or. . . . But many of these people do care about children in general and want public schools to be decent places for children to attend. All adults carry their own experiences in school with them through life. Often these experiences, good or bad, influence how they approach today's schools.

Many senior citizens are involved in politics at the local level. Some attend school board meetings or hold meetings of their own to try to do something about the educational mess we're in. Some consistently fight against schools for one reason or another. When our district had failed to pass a bond to build new schools for eight years, the administration finally decided it was time to involve in the planning process some of the community members who had been voting against us. It wasn't a silver-haired bullet, but it did help the district understand some of the problems and misconceptions that had to be overcome to gain support from more of our senior citizens.

It's time for those of us who want to change things to talk to the friendly neighbor who has no kids in school or the grumpy old man in the back of the boardroom who crabs about his taxes being too high and the number of beater cars lining his street across from the high school from 7:00 to 2:00 every weekday. What do they see that we don't? How do we exchange knowledge and experiences? Golden opportunity!

"Let No Man Despise Thy Youth!"

Often, adults forget to ask students what they think about education. Yet, kids who are offered control over or at least a voice in their own destiny are much more apt to find their own success. Good teachers empower students to take responsibility for learning inside and outside the classroom. As educational activists, it is our responsibility to make sure students are heard and that they understand the struggles to improve their world. One of the best ways to do this is to involve students in our activism and to become involved in theirs. This is easier than it may seem, and, indeed, I'm hoping that some students are reading this book and will continue to reach out to the allies listed above.

When I declared war on WASL testing, I began to find students who were already holding boycotts and practicing peaceful resistance by picketing, writing reports and presentations, and passing out literature. Many junior high and high school students have contacted me for information to include in reports and on websites. Many students who refused to take the tests, in Washington, New York, California, Massachusetts, and several other states, have been in the national news.

I learned recently that there were enough answer sheets turned in with protest essays last year, rather than responses to the actual test questions, that it registered a percentage in the test results here in Washington. I found this out while debating two people who support our state's test. One of the pro-testing participants suggested that teenagers simply goof off and don't take the testing seriously until there are high stakes attached. I countered that our students are doing exactly what we want them to do—thinking on a higher level and deciding that WASL has absolutely no relevance to their lives, academically or otherwise.

Student handbooks have rules about handing out materials during school. Like any other form of activism, there are fine lines and freedoms to consider. Our district "Student Rights" document states that students can distribute "student-generated" information that is approved by the school, as long as it does not cause a disruption in the educational process. Proceed with caution.

My twins took anti-WASL buttons and opt-out sheets that my son had written to school, when they were in seventh grade, and passed them out to friends. I got a call from the principal that day: "Juanita, we have a problem." He said the kids could not hand out anti-WASL supplies during school, because it was causing a disruption. I said we were asking forgiveness rather than permission.

Teaming with our own children or others can be rewarding and educational. When people have suggested that I'm teaching my children to disrespect authority, I say, "Good!" Certainly, if authority is wrong, I want them to question it. I'm raising strong-willed, thoughtful individuals, not compliant drones for the workforce. Cooperation is a good thing only if it serves a good and decent purpose. Mindless conformity has no place in my family, and it should have no place in public schools in a democratic society.

There are student groups throughout the country working on a variety of education issues, from commercialism to diversity to testing. They offer a freshness and enthusiasm to the battlefield that only they can, because they are the only ones who know, personally, how policies affect their education. To experience the sophistication of some of our younger allies, check out <www.nomoretests.com>.

Schools often call students to the office on their eighteenth birthdays to remind them to register to vote. Mark Cortez, an eighteen-year-old high school senior in San Marcos, Texas, took election participation a few steps further recently when he won the approval of his community to be involved with school decision-making on a higher level. By a margin of twenty-one votes, Mark was elected to the school board, for a three-year term. Mark told the *Houston Chronicle,* "I have the point of view of a student, a current student. Most of the board, actually all of the board, haven't been in high school or the school system for a while. I have an inside perspective." That inside perspective should help the board when they hire a new superintendent and attempt to pass a bond issue in the coming year.

It is foolish to attempt to change any education policy, if we have no clue how students feel about it. There are no age barriers for the strategies that follow, but it is important to remember schools are a somewhat controlled environment, which may limit the activism that can take place during school hours. Extracurricular activities, on the other hand, are in!

2   Study Up and Be Prepared

We all know people who are perceived as raving lunatics, and unless we wish to join their ranks in the annals of agitated impotence, we had better learn all we can about our cause, before we begin shouting about it from the steps of the state capitol. "Because I said so!" doesn't go far in winning arguments with three-year-olds or government officials. Both will ask, "Why?" whether they intend to act on your reasoning or not.

Fortunately, there are ample resources available and communication avenues that were not dreamed of even ten to fifteen years ago. The Internet is the activist's friend. If you are thinking of waging any kind of battle with any kind of educational entity and you are not wired, I suggest you get wired—and fast!

Of course there are cheaper ways to begin—the library, for instance, or a work connection—but be prepared to find joining the Internet education community a life-altering experience. The encouragement and person-to-person help in fact-finding available on the web is beyond compare. The up-to-the-minute news, research, and streaming video are indispensable. The most important message, "You are not alone," is worth the price of the computer, the hookup, and the Internet provider.

Not satisfied with the keyboard and screen of it all, I have taken to traveling, meeting my cyber-friends who share my concerns and fighting strategies. Before my Internetworking days, I had never met anyone at the airport by holding up a sign for identification purposes. Now, this is a common occurrence, as I host fellow activists from all over the country and travel to work with and encourage them as well.

In my own area, I often set up meetings and events with Internet contacts. "Meet me at McDonald's on Meridian, Friday. I'm right there for my son's allergy shots anyway, and I'll bring you the graphics and 'Frequently Asked Questions' sheets for your protest."

By now, I may take cyber-connecting with a district superintendent in New York, a researcher in Virginia, and a professor in Kentucky for granted. Nevertheless, it's always exciting to find a friend to work with in my own backyard. I recently found Nancy Vernon, an activist mom, who lives approximately three miles from me, by accessing her website.

Nancy has been investigating the spending habits of the state superintendent by requesting public access files. As is typical of savvy activists, Nancy gathers thorough evidence to make her case *before* taking her concerns to higher authorities or the press. She travels to the state education offices about once a week, carrying along her own portable copy machine. She invited me to come along and see what I could find to help me in my fight against our state's testing. I jumped at the chance. After working together for a few months, Nancy is now finding that my knowledge of testing is helping her with her investigation into state education finances and contracts and special education policy.

There are a couple of lessons here:

1. You don't need to reinvent the wheel. Look for local or national groups or individuals already working on the problem you have just latched onto. Grab the chance to learn from their research.
2. Sometimes advocacy groups make strange bedfellows. You don't have to agree on presidential candidates to show respect for the work and experience of others. Usually people—from professors to PTA treasurers—are happy to share their knowledge.

Beginning at the beginning with a web search is a good idea with any topic or problem, no matter what or whom you may already know.

Enter your topic into <www.google.com> and away you go:

"Searched the web for 'education.' Results 1–10 of about 50,600,000. Search took 0.11 seconds." That's a lot of education in 0.11 seconds. Of course, narrowing your search to specific areas of education is the way to save time and trouble.

"Searched the web for 'high stakes testing.' Results 1–10 of about 96,400. Search took 0.13 seconds."

"Searched the web for 'high stakes testing Texas.' Results 1–10 of about 14,200. Search took 0.38 seconds."

"Searched the web for 'high stakes testing forum Texas.' Results 1–10 of about 3,310. Search took 0.19 seconds."

You get the idea.

Entering names of individuals within the school system or government will usually bring up very interesting links. You may find newspaper articles, government documents, education background, group memberships, etc. If others have researched and placed information on the web, they have probably linked to search engines, saving you time and trouble. Once you become an established activist, which doesn't take long, you may find it interesting to put your own name into the search. I do this occasionally and am sometimes quite surprised to find out who is quoting me where. In fact, even some of my biggest adversaries have been known to quote me in opinion pieces. After which they say they "respectfully disagree." I take that as an admission that I have become a formidable opponent. Thank you, Partnership for Learning—our education reform propaganda specialists in Washington, <www.partnershipfor learning.org>.

A word of warning: be cautious in any assumptions you base on materials found on the Internet. Cheap and easy access to information sharing and publication has its advantages for everyone, including those who do sloppy research or simply like to read their own rantings and ramblings. Check resources and facts carefully and make note of where you read what. Pro and con propaganda and opinion is well tangled on the Internet. The seasoned activist reads all sides and the middle of any issue and keeps the saltshaker, not to mention the delete key, handy.

If you're looking for support and an exchange of ideas and documentations, there are Internet groups of homeschoolers, parents and teachers of children with special needs, those who want to completely separate school from government, those who want old math, new math, vouchers, school choice, straight rows, open class-rooms, phonics, cyber-classrooms, increased parental involvement, a free lunch, and all things beyond and in-between. There are teacher chat boards, parent chat boards, and student chat boards. You can keep up with education coverage from nearly every news-paper and magazine in the world and access reports from regional education laboratories, minutes from state board of education meet-ings, and bills being considered in Congress. Yes, this is the Infor-mation Age. Now you too can compete for bandwidth with your teenage son who is addicted to the latest networked video game.

Some of the best web-sources of help and information can be parents and teachers who have put together websites with the goal of informing and encouraging parents and teachers like themselves.

Two homeschooling moms in Florida, Nance Confer and J.J. Ross, have joined forces to work on the concept of Parent-Directed Education and have created a listserv and website. Nance collects the latest education news and views to share. She writes in her in-troduction, on <*www.parentdirectededucation.org*>, "I want PDE to be a place where we can all speak freely and support each other in finding out more about what our options are or about what they could be—with a lot of hard work."

J.J., whose background includes public school teaching and ad-ministration, adds at the end of her introduction, "Did I mention I have an earned doctorate in education policy and instructional leadership? Big deal. If I can put it to use in your favor, let me know and I'll be glad to try to help. Otherwise, call me J.J., and be sure to disagree with me often to keep me sharp." J.J. writes about issues and answers parent concerns as MisEducation, who is a delightful and informative columnist. Some comments and questions to con-sider from MisEducation:

As new public programs and partnership experiments pop up all over, funded in some pretty "creative" ways, we dubious parents are asking ourselves and each other some very prickly questions.

And it's getting hard to tell who is on which side which day in which state for what reason! Is that philosophy really a peda-gogy dispute? Is this funding fight really about fiscal prudence, or raw power? Is that a credible research report or a political Trojan Horse by guns-for-hire?

The site contains dozens of information links and postings to help parents answer these questions and more for themselves.

Mary Jensen, a teacher in Fresno, California, has created a website <www.teachersmatter.com> to encourage teacher activism. Mary includes a section on "How to become an effective activist," a recommended reading list, and a sample advocacy letter. Three of Mary's suggestions for would-be activists:

- Read reliable research.
- Choose from a variety of advocacy activities that best fit your time constraints.
- Direct your insight in the right direction by using the contact list.

For those in her area, Mary provides an extensive contact list of politicians, media, and organizations.

Beyond web casts and listservs, there are—sometimes more satisfying and often more in-depth—educational publications. Your local bookstore may carry few titles, but searching the library or Internet will reveal many more. Online bookstores such as Amazon <www.Amazon.com> and Barnes and Noble <www.bn.com> have excellent search engines, with which you can find books by topic, author, title, or keywords. They also feature reader reviews, sample pages, author information, and a place to offer your input on the books you have read.

A little time and trouble goes a long way toward finding all the information you can devour. In Appendix 2, I have assembled an emergency stash of web addresses and other resources to get you started or enhance your educational research and meanderings. Included you will find two textbooks. *Educational Administration: Theory, Research, and Practice,* is one I purchased at the local Goodwill for $1. It is now in its sixth edition. I own the fourth. It is an exceptional look at good administrative practice and has provided me a wealth of fighting words over the past year. I emailed one of the authors, Wayne Hoy, and he answered back, encouraging my efforts and giving me names of others who might be able to help me.

Teaching Strategies, A Guide to Better Instruction, was given to me by its author, Dr. Donald Orlich, professor emeritus at Washington State University. As he told me, once I read it cover to cover, I will know more about teaching than the best-informed educrat. These suggestions are provided as examples of the sound foundation of information necessary for serious, successful activism.

A good way to grow a library is to browse the college textbook and education bookshelves of second-hand stores, library sales, etc. For a few dollars you can own several slightly worn, still worthwhile volumes. Add to these, Internet access and a few books on current education concerns and you will be well armed with facts, figures, insight, and quotable quotes. It may also be helpful to subscribe to an education journal or two, such as *Phi Delta Kappan* <www.pdkintl.org/kappan/kappan.htm> or *ASCD Journal (Association for Supervision and Curricular Development)* <www.ascd.org> just to keep up on current issues and ideas in the inner circles of the education world. Some articles from journals can be found online, but others are in print form only.

Knowing the answer to a question before you ask it of an official has long been a rule of thumb for courtroom lawyers and grassroots activists. It tells us whether someone can be trusted or whether they have things to hide. It makes us look better than many politicians or educrats, who trust assistants to do their legwork and, sometimes, most of their thinking.

Just Ask Them

As education reform is bestowed on us as the do-all, be-all of school structure, it becomes necessary to question each piece of the new world order, so that we don't throw out any possible merit that new ideas have to offer.

To avoid hearing worthless, canned responses, it is good to approach education leaders with well-planned questioning strategies that require them to think on the spot about just how their plans will affect real children living in real homes and attending real classrooms.

Participate in information meetings with a group of friends, each armed with one or two questions. If you are not satisfied with the answers you receive on the spot, follow up in writing and send the questions to all leaders involved in the decision to use the new concept or policy. While asking questions and getting answers, try to discern from whom or where the new ideas are coming. This will give you an idea of what you may be up against and who you must approach, if you see problems with the changes being made.

Questioning the Authority of Reform

1. What does the new concept mean, really? Could you explain that, please?
2. Are there statistics available to support the plan, or will my child/the children in my school be a test case?
3. What benefits will this program have?
4. Will the new teaching strategy reach all children equally, or will it need to be modified for some?
5. If the new program is designed to meet the needs of only certain students, are there equally effective programs in place for other students?
6. Are teachers and assistants adequately trained in the new concept?
7. What is the cost of the program, and does the expected improvement warrant the time and money that will be needed to implement it?
8. Is there a current program that is already serving the assumed need adequately?
9. Will the necessary evaluations be carried out every few months, or when appropriate, to assure that the new program or strategy is successful, worthwhile, and educationally sound?
10. Will those involved be willing to make adjustments, if necessary, or reverse or discontinue the plan, if it is found to be unsuccessful or to lack staff or parent support?
11. Has the program been tried in other schools? Are the other schools still utilizing the program? Was it successful? How do we know this?
12. Are options available for parents, teachers, and students who do not agree with or believe in the new concept?

© 2003 Juanita Doyon from *Not With Our Kids You Don't*. Portsmouth, NH: Heinemann

---

Figure 2–1 Reform Questions

3

Look in the Mirror at the End of the Day

In the best interest of educrats everywhere, teachers and parents are continually pitted against each other. When school bus runs are cut back and six-year-olds have to walk a mile to the bus stop or when school lunch menus offer rock-hard waffles or when math books contain mistakes teachers are the first to hear parent complaints and the last to be able to fix the problem. Things like big stacks of test-prep homework dittos can drive a wedge between parents and teachers. Sometimes it doesn't take much in an unforgiving world for the *education partners* to begin separation proceedings. Can this relationship be saved? I believe it can, if teachers and parents can find a way to work honestly together, despite demands from above.

Recently, in California, a court ruled that it is lawful for teachers to inform parents that they may opt their children out of SAT 9 assessments. The testing regulation used to read: "A parent or guardian may submit to the school a written request to excuse his or her child from any or all parts of any test provided pursuant to Education Code section 60640. The parent or guardian must initiate the request and the school district and its employees shall not solicit or encourage any written request on behalf of any child."

Thanks to the court settlement of a lawsuit between the San Francisco School District and the state, the state school board modified the rule to include the statement, "A school district and its employees may discuss the STAR program with parents and may inform parents of the availability of exemptions." Teachers do have rights—at least in California—if they know about them. The California Department of Education has not done much to get news of the change out to districts, and, when last I checked, the statement had not yet been added to the Education Code on the CDE website. Districts are still advising teachers that they are not to inform parents of opt-out rights.

Franci Benson, a parent in Washougal, Washington, picketed her school district office to protest WASL testing. Franci's daughter Ashley, frustrated that her teachers don't like the WASL testing but feel helpless to make change, made a poster for the event, stating simply, "Freedom of Speech, Teachers Have Rights Too!"

Some states, such as Colorado and Washington, average a zero into the school percentage scores for students who are not tested. California refuses to give test score bonus money to districts with a 10 or 15 percent opt-out rate—depending on what source of information is used. And in many states, it is illegal for parents to opt their children out of testing in the first place.

Michelle Trusty-Murphy, of Minden, Nevada, was served truancy papers for keeping her ten-year-old son, Connor, home during testing. Michelle had requested that Connor not be tested, but the school refused to honor her request. Each time Connor returned to school, the principal took him to a room and put a make-up test in front of him. Finally, Connor drew a line down the bubble-in columns, telling the principal that he was finished taking the test. Test security requires that only one answer sheet be given to each student. The principal was forced to accept the line as Connor's final answer.

The high-stakes testing coercion continues. Parental rights and good administrative policy often get brushed aside in the quest for test scores. Students are sometimes threatened with class failure and lowered grades, even in states where opt-out is legal. Teachers are told by principals to phone parents who have sent opt-out notes and convince them to allow their children to take the tests.

My nephew Nathan Lamont decided with his mother that he would not take the tenth-grade WASL. He was told by his English teacher that the writing section of the state test would count toward his class grade and that the school was awarding high school credits to students who pass sections of the WASL—one-quarter credit for each of the four sections passed. We are questioning the district and voicing concerns about this policy in a state where parents may legally opt their children out of the state test. One of the favorite phrases used by leaders to justify high-stakes testing is that we need a "diploma that means something." Perhaps they want it to mean that kids passed a test in tenth grade to gain extra credits without doing any class work for them.

Donna Hippensteal, a parent in my own district, wrote a note to exempt her son from WASL testing at one of our district's two high schools. Before testing began, Donna had to leave town to attend her grandmother's funeral. While she was gone, the school principal, in possession of the parent-signed exemption, convinced the son that he should take the test, rather than take part in the alternative activities. When she returned from the family emergency, Donna and I paid a visit to the principal, who had trouble understanding why Donna was upset. Donna made it clear that she did not want WASL results in her son's record. However, when scores came out in the fall, she received them in the mail anyway. She is still trying to decide what course of action to take. When she attempted to get her son's scores from the school, to make sure they were not in his permanent record, they could not be found.

It would seem that between educationally consenting adults there would always be room for honesty. Sadly this isn't the case. Every school day, teachers do and say things that they "have to" in order to keep the peace and their jobs. When administrative policy is state-mandated and top-down, there is little room for honest parent/teacher collaboration. And when parent/teacher collaboration breaks down, the most involved and capable parents tend to flee the school or the entire system. This leaves teachers, students, and schools with less community support.

Sometimes those in district communications positions can be quite attention deficit when it comes to communicating with parents. Sadly, teachers and parents are stuck to deal with lack-of-trust issues when district officials are insincere and condescending.

Jean Ward is a friend and fellow parent activist in my area. While emailing back and forth with her district administration about WASL and the new math curriculum, something very sad—

MY CHILD IS NOT YOUR DATA

Figure 3–1 My Child Is Not Your Data

yet comical—happened. The district person in charge of communications replied to an email, hitting the "reply all" key, rather than forwarding to another district official. Jean received a message asking who got to "spin the wheel" and win the task of answering the cranky parent's email. Needless to say, those of us in the parenting circle have had more than a few laughs over that one. I don't suppose the person who hit the wrong button on the keyboard felt particularly amused when she realized she had shown her true attitude to a parent who is quite sophisticated in communications and never skimps when it comes to investigating a situation.

Parents and teachers should realize that officials who are aloof and disrespectful to parents more than likely hold the same attitude toward teachers and vice versa. Educational empathy between those closest to children makes the battle worth bearing and helps secure quality education in most cases.

When parents ask teachers how they truly feel about situations, support is demonstrated. When teachers share their honest opinions with parents, trust is instilled. Some situations that can open communication channels are parent/teacher conferences, PTA meetings, and school-sponsored events. Field-trip busses are great places for room moms and dads to get to know teachers. Very interesting discussions can take place while the kids are chanting "Who Stole the Cookie from the Cookie Jar" for the fifty-seventh time on the way to the theater to see the live staging of *The Nutcracker.* (A little tip, it is part of the show for the fifth-grade audience to fall asleep in the second act.) From the inner circle, word ripples easily to other parents and teachers that "our concerns are your concerns."

Beyond intimate parent/teacher conversations, it can be economically dangerous for teachers and other school personnel to speak out against the hand that feeds and clothes them. Only you can prevent reprimands, write-ups, and punch-in-the-gut, after-school announcements, "*crackle . . . crackle . . . crackle . . .* Ms. Loudmouth, Mr. Crankybottom would like to see you in his office immediately! Bring your backpack, ready to go home." Uh-oh!

Remember though, there are worse things than reprimands and there is no better cause than educational justice for which to collect them. Just because taking a stand can involve high stakes doesn't mean that you shouldn't carefully proceed to the nearest soapbox. There are usually ways to protect yourself from serious consequences.

At University Hill Elementary School, in Boulder, Colorado, teachers organized a fast and encouraged others to join them, to bring attention to the issue of high-stakes testing. The teachers planned to donate money saved on meals to the Foundation for Boulder Valley Schools. Listed in their concerns about the tests were the costs—$14.5 million for administration plus the cost of teacher and student time that could be better spent—and the discriminatory nature of the tests to second language learners and children from low socioeconomic backgrounds. In their announcement of the activism event, the organizing teachers, Dara Glazer and Jeff Oliver, included the following points from the district union president and assistant superintendent:

- The district position is they will neither condemn nor condone this action as long as we abide by our contracts.
- This action should not negatively affect or impact our students. We should not involve them in any way.
- We cannot do any of this during contract hours.
- This cannot affect your ability to carry out your job, i.e., if you pass out due to hunger.

Unless you walk on water, test it before you jump in, particularly if you like your paid position, are not tenured, or have a

Figure 3–2 Stop CSAP

vindictive, "toe the company/state/bureaucracy line" chain of command hanging over your head—and who doesn't, at one level or another, these days?

Know your building, your district, and your state. Know your union representative and your union board; make sure they know you and your motives. Whenever possible use the channeling approach first:

- See if your union representative agrees with you.
- See if your state and/or professional association has taken a written stand on the issue.
- See if parents with big mouths and sharp keyboards share your concerns.
- Watch for letters to the editor in your local paper.

A bandwagon is always safer—and louder—than a bicycle towing a banner.

When I was in kindergarten, my dad would take me to the library often. One favorite book that we checked out several times was *If Everybody Did* by Jo Ann Stover. On one page is a picture of one person doing something undesirable. On the facing page are the exaggerated consequences: "This is what would happen if everybody did." My favorite page was always, "Squeeze the cat," with the resulting hourglass-shaped feline. There is something about the lessons in childhood reading that sticks with people through life. The last example in the book has each person doing the right thing, which adds up to everybody doing the right thing. Now, let's apply that to education.

- How do teachers and parents find a common place to work for educational justice?
- How do we find forgiveness, empathy, and honesty to replace combativeness and confrontation?

Ask and answer the questions and follow the simple rules in Figures 3–3 and 3–4 and together teachers and parents will rock the education world!

School Rules for Parents

1. Never assume. Get the facts.
2. Maintain a sense of humor at all times.
3. Read all paperwork as promptly as possible.
4. Save newsletters, etc., until they are out of date.
5. Keep a phone list of schools, PTA officers, school board members, parents in your child's school, and district central office staff.
6. Subscribe to the daily newspaper and read it.
7. Vote in all elections.
8. Get to know a few parents in your child's school.
9. Meet the teacher and principal before you have to.
10. If you have Internet access, bookmark district and state websites, and find out about email accessible updates from teachers and schools.
11. Find a way to show your appreciation for school staff.

Figure 3–3 School Rules for Parents (in No Particular Order of Importance)

School Rules for Teachers

1. Never assume. Get the facts.
2. Maintain a sense of humor at all times.
3. Read all paperwork as promptly as possible.
4. Save newsletters, etc., until they are out of date.
5. Keep a phone list of schools, PTA officers, school board members, and district central office staff. Share these liberally with parents.
6. Subscribe to the daily newspaper and read it.
7. Vote in all elections.
8. Meet and get to know the parents in your school before you have to.
9. If appropriate for your community, utilize email and web pages to communicate with parents. Use web sources to keep up to date with district and state education policy.
10. Find a way to show your appreciation for parents.

Figure 3–4 School Rules for Teachers (in No Particular Order of Importance)

Moonlight Activism

Teresa Glenn teaches eighth-grade language arts in North Carolina. When Teresa was confronted by standardized testing week, with the choice to administer the test or lose her job, she asked for help in reconciling herself to the situation from members of the Assessment Reform Network listserv. This is a national group of test resisters in association with FairTest, the organization for fair and open testing, <*www.fairtest.org*>.

The several responses Teresa received assured her that our schools need dedicated teachers, particularly during these times that test our kids and our souls. The parents among us assured her that we would rather have someone who understood the evils of the tests with our kids on testing day than someone who believed in all this junk. Teresa fulfilled her duty, assisting a student with special accommodations during testing. In her own words, from an email on the morning of testing: "I'm taking my student my own lucky rabbit's foot, which accompanied me to my SATs and all major exams, and I'm taking myself an extra-expensive cup of coffee."

It isn't always possible to follow our convictions completely where we work and live. As a school employee or a parent, it can be easier and less frustrating to take on an injustice outside or beyond your own school or district. I've been extremely fortunate to almost always have my own children in schools and with teachers I knew were doing a good job despite the incessant assessment insanity swirling around them. This has given me the freedom to act on the district, state, and national level.

If you are reasonably comfortable with your own school, or even if there are problems, but you don't feel you can act on them at the moment, try looking beyond the specks temporarily to break up a logjam. If you don't feel like arguing with your own principal who is pushing you to teach that rote reading formula by script, start petitioning the state board about curriculum adoption practices. Think big and anonymous rather than up close and personal. Take a look at the state and national situation, or look at a neighboring district. Chances are there are problems, similar to what you may be experiencing, going on wherever you choose to look.

Consider the reform propagandists—raking in the dough—who have been imported for professional development, and ask yourself how you can utilize this visiting prophet strategy to improve your situation. Throughout the *restructuring process* our district has taken *teams* from buildings for day-long *strategic planning* or, sometimes, during the winter doldrums, to hear motivational speakers. If you find several people interested in working on a problem, why not plan an agitator's retreat to advance your cause? This could entail hiring a professional presenter or it could be as cheap and easy as finding a concerned parent or teacher—call them a "local activist"—in your own or a nearby district, who is willing to present or lead a brainstorming session on your topic of concern.

There are public, off-campus meeting places available in every community, many of them for free. These can include churches, granges, libraries, and community centers. In these places, teachers, parents, and others can network and create plans for action.

One way that some teachers have chosen to be good examples of activism to their communities is to use their status as parent to join the opt-out or boycott cause. Corinne McOmber teaches first grade in Connecticut. At the risk of legal consequences, Corinne refused to allow her two daughters to take the Connecticut Mastery

Figure 3–5 My Kid Puked on Your High Stakes Test!

Tests in the fall of 2001. She also wrote and collected more than 200 signatures on a petition to change state testing policy to legalize opt-outs and improve rules for English language learners. The petition was presented to members of the state legislative education committee at a forum on state testing.

There is power in the sheer numbers of teachers, parents, and students in our country. If enough teachers begin to speak up and take action or encourage the action of parents, there is great hope for the future of our public schools. This may be a long-range thought and may not bring much comfort to those in more oppressive or depressing areas, but those who are employed in places that truly value quality education do have a chance to bring about meaningful change in policy for all of us.

In the spring of 2001, parents in Scarsdale, NY, held a boycott of the state's eighth-grade Regents Exams. For their trouble, the Scarsdale district was investigated by the state education department, to see that attendance laws and testing protocol had been followed. School staff had let parents know that they were administering the tests only because they had to follow state law. They did not take time out of regular lessons for test preparation.

The PTA invited standardized test critic, activist, and author Alfie Kohn <*www.alfiekohn.org*> to speak, and, in a principal's newsletter, parents were encouraged to attend. Parents petitioned the school board to direct the school administration to cancel the tests. However, required to follow state law, the school board informed parents that the tests would be administered as scheduled.

Parents planned the boycott carefully so that students would miss only times that the actual tests were to be given. They set up carpools to pick up students and return them to school when testing was over for the day. The first day of testing, out of 290 eighth graders, only 95 were tested. The boycott continued and was successful throughout the testing period and during makeup tests, as news of the boycott spread throughout the country.

After a thorough investigation by the state, a letter of reprimand was sent to Scarsdale Superintendent Michael V. McGill, from State Education Commissioner Richard P. Mills, requiring the district to submit and follow a plan to encourage 100 percent participation on future state exams. No matter what the outcome of these recommendations and requirements on the district, the boycott in Scarsdale encouraged test resistance throughout New York and around the country, not just for one year, but in all future years that test resistance is necessary.

Those of us fighting standardized test abuse keep track of successful protests and boycotts. We watch and listen and learn from what works. Educational activists need each other, no matter what the fight. Teachers and parents need to know that there are others out there pulling for them, having the same experiences, and feeling the same frustrations. The school board of Scarsdale has since passed a statement on testing and assessment. This document outlines the shortcomings of high-stakes testing. One of its well-written statements:

> Mass testing and related public pressure may improve scores. They can sometimes force under-performing schools or teachers to focus on clearer objectives. However, they also have undesirable consequences, narrowing instruction to only what might be tested and prompting an excessive emphasis on test preparation. This narrowing and flattening of education is the antithesis of the deep, rich, engaging learning that should be the goal of all schools. The problem occurs more in the case of academic content than of skills. Therefore, mass testing should be limited to the areas of math, reading, and writing.
> *From* <http://www.scarsdaleschools.k12.ny.us/statement.html>

As Scarsdale administers Regents Exams in future years, under the ever-watchful eye of the State Department of Education, those

of us who have gained encouragement from their success will return to them the encouragement to carry on in the face of strong
opposition. For each of us, there is a time to be brave and to show
that we are willing to live with the consequences of our convictions.
As Ghandi said, "First they ignore you; then they laugh at you; then
they fight you; then you win." Investigations, reprimands, and mandatory consequences for student absences: our opponents are fighting us. Next we win!

If my national networking has taught me one important thing,
it's that there is nothing new or unique behind any schoolhouse
door. Problems may differ in intensity; resources may vary; but the
makeup of education is human kids, parents, teachers, administrators, and community members. If left to work it out and utilize reasonable resources, I have just enough faith in my fellow Americans
to believe that things would be okay for the majority of kids and
adults in our public schools. Under the thumb and the poor spending and administrative policies of our state and national govern-
ments, our schools will continue to deteriorate, while they struggle
to deal with the inequities and the societal problems around and
within them.

A Good Rant . . .

I'm currently embroiled in an ugly power struggle with an
insensitive, anti-union, "forgot-how-much-work-it-is-to-be-a-
teacher-as-soon-as-he-became-a-principal," management drone
who piles on so much "fluff" busy-work in the name of education reform that if we teachers want to fashion effective lessons
we must do it on our own time. I'll have to tell you how I *really*
feel about him, sometime! It's also report card weekend—a
weekend when I, as well as most teachers I know, will put in
twelve to twenty hours at home, on our own time, unpaid, preparing report cards. Heaven forbid we teachers ever be allowed
any company time to perform this piece of company work!

Then you have a week of parent conferences, often running
into the evening hours. You go into each conference wondering
if this will be the one where the parent arrives drunk or angry
or both! Will you be expected to referee a fight between a cus-
todial and a non-custodial parent? If their child's not doing
well, how will they try to twist it so that it comes out to be your
fault? (It's never through any fault of the child, anymore!) Will

they even arrive at all or will they just stand you up? (I'll tell you a little secret about teacher conferences: We teachers know exactly why the kid is the way s/he is, within 30 seconds of the time the parent(s) first walk in the classroom door! Scary, eh?) But, thank God, most of the parents are good supportive people and most of the conferences turn out to be a good stimulating exchange of information, enjoyable and even fun!

—*dedicated fourth-grade teacher*

On-site Activism

Of course some of us involved in education are blessed to have found our activism niche in a paying position. As I've struggled to define activism in the trenches, it has occurred to me that nearly every person employed by our school system is an activist in at least some small way—even if it is only to improve the life of one child. I think of a program in my own school, developed by teachers Theresa Lee-Hodson and Tom Cruver, where students who are otherwise lost in the system work to improve their reading, math, and social studies skills while they are also given the opportunity to run a catering service, the Bulldog Express.

The county health department comes to the school to administer the program required for food-handling permits. Students learn cooking and serving procedures and provide refreshments for many district functions, from award ceremonies to faculty meetings.

Another part of the program, Community Ventures, allows students to make kimonos for premature babies, lap robes for people in nursing homes, and hats for cancer patients. These items are shared with local hospitals and an "adopted" nursing home.

Every February, the Bulldog Express puts on a community dinner in the junior high cafeteria. With donated food from stores and restaurants, they prepare and serve a free dinner to hundreds of parents, teachers, and senior citizens, who receive special invitations or find out about the dinner from the school reader-board. A great variety of food is served to three shifts of guests, who begin arriving at 4:00 P.M. and have all been served by 7:00 P.M.

Each year, the school receives thank you notes from several adults who attend the dinner. Invariably, one of these notes will say that these students are some of the most respectful and hardworking young people the person has been exposed to in a long time and a good example for others. The students do an excellent job with this and all the events they cater. Integrating learning with life and making it real, the teachers who have built this program are changing the world for their students—activism at its finest!

Within the system, there are schools and districts that honor freedom of thought and open expression of opinion. Professional journals and education association websites have many official statements that go against the status quo. Many school board members and administrators do their best to speak out and encourage others to do so as well. Some schools have open-forum bulletin boards in their staff lounges. I happened to be making copies of WASL war materials one day when I met up with a teacher I know. I gave her a copy of the packet I was putting together to distribute at a state education conference. She said she would post it on the information board at school.

Colleges, high schools, and junior highs have newspapers, run by students, which can be an outlet for activism encouragement. The editor of the student newspaper at Bethel High School—coincidentally, my alma mater—interviewed me last year during testing season. I also supplied her with graphics for her article. As caring citizens, we must use or lose our freedom of speech within our schools—not as manipulation of our subordinates to join our cause, but to encourage open discussion and thought.

Many colleges offer classes that encourage activism. Recently, Peg Tysver, who teaches a class on standardized testing at Evergreen State College's Tacoma campus, contacted me. She had assigned her classes an activism project of their choosing. One of her students, Candy Benteu, arranged for me to come and present to the morning class. The evening class requested that I be part of a debate/discussion panel they set up, with two people who were in favor of our state's WASL testing.

The name of the two classes I worked with was "Testing, Tracking, and De Facto Segregation." I was in the right place! The vision statement of this particular campus, which is located on the edge of Tacoma's culturally diverse and economically challenged Hilltop district, is "Enter to learn. Depart to serve." Education begets a lifetime of activism. Because many of the students come from communities that have been impacted by the discriminatory education policy they study, their sense of social and educational justice is perhaps more keen than that of students on the average college campus. Gaining the knowledge and ability to inform and help those in one's own community is powerful activism.

Fallen Apples

Brave, outspoken teachers are not often featured on the golden apple award segment of local TV stations, but in the field of teacher activists there are many, throughout the country, who deserve a Red Apple of Courage. When teachers speak out or take action, helping expose the truth or right a wrong, against the odds of continued employment and security, they deserve praise from colleagues and leaders alike. Instead, what they often get is ridicule and economic hardship handed down from the powers that live to be arrogant and controlling, and they are often shunned by colleagues who fear reproof by association.

I include the following stories, not to discourage the prospective activist, but to inspire courage in the face of the adversity. It is most often the exceptional, adventurous educator we seek to emulate, so it is the extraordinary, risk-taking educational activist we should uphold.

George Schmidt used to be a well-experienced high school English teacher at Bowen High School in Chicago. He also served as gang security coordinator and his school's Chicago Teacher's Union delegate. In January 1999, George made the decision to publish the Chicago CASE tests in *Substance* newspaper, a monthly education publication he helped to start in 1975. George wanted to expose the idiotic content and poor quality of the tests. Though the tests had already been administered to students, the Chicago school board chose to sue Mr. Schmidt and *Substance* for copyright damages amounting to what they claimed to be $1.3 million. George was also dismissed from his long-time teaching position.

I asked George, who is now editing *Substance* full-time and working to build his defense against the school district's charges, if, in retrospect, he would publish the tests again or do anything differently. His answers, "Yes," he would publish the test and "No," he would not do anything differently. As he explains it, he was following first amendment rights and doing what any newspaper is meant to do—exposing government "craziness and waste." George Schmidt believes, as many of us in the test-resistance believe, that any test given to children in our public schools should be openly and completely available for public viewing immediately after administration. There should be no secret tests in a free country.

In Birmingham, Alabama, Steve Orel began questioning the "administrative dismissal" of 522 students from Birmingham high schools. The students had been involuntarily removed from school just before the administration of SAT 9 tests, for showing, as many of their dismissal papers noted, a "lack of interest" in academic pursuits. Birmingham schools were under pressure to increase test scores or be taken over by the state. Surely, the test scores of these students would not improve the district average.

As Mr. Orel studied the issue and discovered the reasoning behind the student dismissals, he wrote a term paper for a graduate course he was taking. With help from two school board members, the situation was brought to light in the press. Steve began to feel pressure from district administration, who questioned him about the term paper he had written and asked if he had received permission before speaking with the press.

Steve's own words from the Interversity website tell best how his teaching position with the Birmingham school district ended:

> I asked and received permission to speak at a Board meeting, at which time I presented a proposal to retrieve the withdrawn students and get them back into an intense reading remediation program at their respective schools. The Board gave me three minutes to present my views. What was their response? I was terminated by Birmingham City Schools the next day.
> <www.interversity.com/events/resisting_conf/texts/Orel7488.php>

Steve Orel now works as assistant director and lead teacher at the World of Opportunity, an agency that offers adult education and job awareness. Many of the students who were pushed out of Birmingham schools for "lack of interest" have found their way to this program and worked hard to receive their General Equivalency Diploma. Steve shares the successes of World of Opportunity students with the Assessment Reform Network quite often.

Would Steve follow his convictions again, even if he knew it meant the loss of his job? More of his own words from the Interversity website: "From the very outset, I was cautioned by administrators within the academic and teaching community that my job would not survive bringing these revelations to the light of day. But I knew that I was speaking the truth and I was duty-bound to defend our students. There seemed no choice to me but to speak the truth, stand beside the students I worked with, and try to put an end to this standardized test-driven madness."

A Call for Accountability

During conference week—this week—I had one parent tell me that she was thinking of putting her son in private school "because they don't have to do the WASL." A grandmother said today she believed a lot of students will drop out of high school in order not to have to take the WASL. It probably was one of you who searched out where I taught and contacted my district, because of the letters I've written to you. That was not a very nice thing to do—let alone professional. The person you contacted should have been outraged that a public person would use their available information to search me out and tattle to my administration. I don't care, because I am on the right side. You are destroying education with your WASL. One thing good is that the parents whose children are going to be affected by the 10th grade WASL are finally waking up and forming groups. You didn't listen to teachers so maybe you will listen to parents.

—emailed to Washington State's Academic Achievement and Accountability Commission, by a brave fourth-grade teacher

STRATEGY

Plan Carefully, Think Ahead, and Secure Your Own Oxygen Mask Before Assisting Others

Playing the Numbers

For me, the interaction made possible by Internet access was natural and easy, but there comes a point in any kind of school improvement campaign when further outreach requires some sort of get-together or person-to-person word spreading. This means activities such as petition drives, forums, door-to-door solicitations, or visiting and signing in at PTA or other meetings to broadcast your concerns. Where and how to seek support depends completely on the cause for which you are fighting.

When our district made plans to charge every student $50 for band participation, I took a petition to band classes, where I knew the teachers, explained the situation to the junior and senior high students, and gave them the opportunity to sign. In one afternoon, the signatures of 300 students were added to my petition, which I presented to the school board that evening, making sure to point out that I was missing my son's final band concert of the year in order to be at the board meeting—always make the most of every situation.

In retrospect, soliciting student signatures during class time may not have been completely appropriate, but it was completely successful. The board decided that an activity fee would be charged only for extracurricular, after-school activities, not cocurricular classes. Well-meaning parents can sometimes work wonders cautiously walking the edge of propriety.

Activists are constantly playing a game of numbers. Poor, grass-roots activists—which most educational activists are—must learn to plan well, utilize free advertising, and never, and I mean *never,* be disappointed at a small turnout to an event.

One of the first things members of the media ask, when being told about an event or cause, is, "How many people are involved?" Overestimating the number of people who are in a group or attending an event can damage your reputation. Underestimating can cause lack of interest on the part of the press. My best advice when publicizing the human resource volume of your association is:

- Be vague
- Be conservative
- Be creative
- All of the above

My "Mothers Against WASL" organization is a "loose-knit, Internet-based community of child advocates." I don't know how many parents and teachers are in the group, because all those who contact me reach out to others in their own areas. When writing a press release for the Mothers and Others Walk Against WASL, I said I was expecting a small turnout, as this was our first organized event. The thirty people who took part were a "well-concentrated group from communities throughout the Puget Sound." You see, without hiring a press agent or an advertising company, we can make ourselves quite presentable and even impressive to the media and the public. Well-presented small groups will become larger and more powerful.

Making the most of a planned event, such as a corner rally or educational forum, depends on a well-prepared attitude and acceptance of "whatever happens, happens." Mickey VanDerwerker is a mother of five in Virginia. She is a former Teacher of the Year and a current member of two school boards. Mickey also leads the charge

Figure 4–1 Mothers Against WASL

against her state's high-stakes testing system. Her clear and simple advice for planning committees of test resistance? "Don't meet."

One of the first forums planned by the Virginia test resistance was attended by Ms. VanDerwerker and the press—period. Thinking on her feet, as all great activists learn to do, Mickey made an announcement and apologized to the assembled press. "The meeting has been cancelled and will be rescheduled at a later date."

Time and Talent

In this double- and triple-duty world, most of us operate with a fine balance of commitment to family, work, friends, and service organizations. Not many of us have time to set up a brand-new, regular meeting schedule and clear the stacks of papers from the living room to sit around like the vultures in Disney's *Jungle Book,* asking, "Well, what we gonna do?" State boards of education, accountability commissions, and business roundtables make far better vultures, and these groups all meet quite regularly.

If you should happen to enjoy planning coffee klatches, and you happen to be or know a well-organized-mover-and-shaker-facilitator-with-a-plan, go for it. Just remember, it takes a lot of charisma to draw a crowd of exhausted teachers or parents to a planning meeting on a school and work night, much less a coveted

Saturday morning or afternoon. I find it best to reserve energy for forums and protests and do the planning on the run or on the computer. Email it. Phone it in. Delegate it through the mail. But don't waste time planning to make plans. Life is too short.

When networking well with others, try to multitask. Use preset meetings to communicate face to face. Often, my closest protesting buddy and I will dream and scheme as we sit at the back of a state accountability meeting. There are plenty of dull moments in these, when the commission members aren't fighting amongst themselves, that we can put to good use sharing notes and lists. If supply exchanges are needed, this is a good time for that too—saves postage and gas. If we are too busy during the meeting taking notes or preparing to present, we can always go to lunch afterward and do a little brainstorming or firming up of details on an upcoming activity.

If you find it absolutely necessary to schedule a meeting of your own, at least serve the purpose of bodily nourishment at the same time, by meeting for breakfast, lunch, or dinner. Keep meetings timely, well organized, and successful by bringing a list of points to discuss and decisions to make.

- SET a time limit
- STICK to an agenda
- GO away with a "what next" action plan

There are no guarantees that the allies we find in our struggles will be able to offer great things to the cause. In fact, when thinking of what others can offer, it is best not to expect much; then we won't be disappointed. Most of us are so busy with our own families and work that any moments away are considered grand theft by our spouse or our kids. There is only so much neglect any family should have to put up with in the name of educational justice. Sure, they're proud of us—to a point.

When I say I'm a "full-time activist," I actually mean I'm obsessed. My family is extremely understanding; my husband hardly ever throws a fit about the cluttered house or the lack of a decent meal. But I don't expect the people who are willing to work with me to enter this state of dysfunction in their daily lives.

I have a mug that a friend gave me. The inscription is from a saying on the blackboard of the Vergennes School House in a

Vermont museum. "Nothing is work, unless you would rather be doing something else." I love what I'm doing most of the time, but there are times when I should be doing something else. Many people couldn't set things aside as I do and stay sane. I realize this. I also try to remember my own limits and do a few dishes every now and then, cook a meal, wash clothes, and order my kids around to help me get things to an acceptable state of order. There is, after all, a fine line between devotion and dementia, when it comes to any "cause."

As you begin to network, you will need to decide just how far you want to go with different associations. The best gauge for me has been a gut feeling I have for when to join and when to simply help, when to sign on as a candidate or when to help others running for the office. The best way I can think of to describe it is soul searching.

In my life, I have worked on two types of political campaigns, both having to do with education. School bond and levy campaigns to build schools or run the district at a decent level of service were my first political action, which I began as a junior in high school. My friends and I would get my dad to drive us around in his Ford Ranchero truck while we waved signs and yelled through a megaphone to friends and neighbors, "Vote yes, Bethel schools!" I've worked on several of these campaigns as an adult. Often they are quite frustrating, as the supermajority requirement in Washington causes the always over 50-percent but often under 60-percent "yes" vote to be a horrible letdown.

My second type of campaign work began when I found there were four challengers for the position of state superintendent in the fall 2000 election. I knew I had to help them somehow, so I found out as much as I could about each, worked on some graphics and word spreading and did my best to get the votes away from the incumbent. When the current superintendent won in the primary with more than 50 percent but less than 60 percent of the vote—if she had been a bond or levy she would have failed—and didn't even have to campaign for the final election, it was extremely frustrating.

Just after the election, someone made the suggestion that I run for superintendent next time—then four years away. I did a lot of that soul searching I mentioned. Then I asked the advice of friends, family, coactivists, and scholars. Many concerns were expressed and much advice given. Though I'm still laughing at myself, it seems like the right thing to do. I have registered with my state public-disclosure commission and have become an official part of the campaign for educational justice—as a candidate. Heaven help me!

The opportunity to join with others or have others join with you may present itself continuously, particularly if you are friendly, outgoing, and enthusiastic about your cause. If you find that there is good help in your area and feel that your fight will be long and steady, you may want to consider forming a nonprofit organization. Another alternative is to work under the security of a nonprofit group that already exists. This can be done easily, if an established group is willing to oversee your financial dealings.

There are time and trouble pros and cons to being "official," and there are legal considerations, which are state specific and also covered by federal laws. An excellent web resource with answers to nonprofit questions can be found at <www.nonprofits.org>. There you will find dozens of topics to dig into, under the headings "Organization, Management, Regulation, Resources, and Development." The site covers everything from board-staff relations to sample conflict of interest policies to celebrity fundraising. If a nonprofit needs to know, it seems to be there. Other websites of nonprofit information can be found in Appendix 2.

Knowing our limits is a life-preserving skill. A willingness to accept the help of others is another. Any amount of time or talent that people can offer is welcome. Any work or word-spreading is a help. Often, people are very willing to help with finances, paying for buttons or shirts and giving them away to others. I often mail flyers and posters for others to make copies and distribute. Some people are willing to plan an event in their communities, if I'm able to come and speak or help. It serves us well to remember that activism is a voluntary activity. We are always free to "Just Say No."

Preachers Within the Choir and Other Time Wasters

As much as I love the Internet contacts I have made in the past year, I always have to be on my guard for the stagnation of congratulatory email clubs or the exhaustive water treading brought about by single-minded jerks looking for a debate team to join. If I'm doing nothing to truly inform people or spur them into action, I will get into a rut. Ruts are not productive places. Ruts can keep me spinning my wheels.

Internet sociology is a fascinating field for study. Internet bullies, time wasters, gadflies, and whiners: all have their place alongside many very positive people who are seeking meaningful discussion or help with problems or sources of information.

If you find yourself in the middle of a conversation you didn't anticipate or are uncomfortable with, by all means, opt out! If you find the addiction to email cramping your real life, sign off the list for a while.

In many lists, the same conversation is held in an endless cycle, popping up at least once every few months. In one listserv I belong to, it's whether religion has any place in public school. In another, it's whether grades have any place in public school. Both discussions are something that almost everyone can paint an eloquent personal opinion about, but nobody will ever really change the mind of anyone else on either of these topics. Unless your creative writing skills need sharpening or you absolutely can't think of anything else to do with your time and talent, it's best to avoid these kinds of high-fallutin', omnipresent philosophical discussions.

Computer-accessed communication is superior in some ways and inferior in others to phone conversations and face-to-face meetings. Becoming an efficient user of technology is a great asset to activism. Honing communication skills is the key to progress. Just remember to take inventory every now and then, to see if your communications and alliances, both online and off, are having a positive impact on your efforts or the efforts of others. It sometimes becomes necessary to bow out or sign off gracefully. Never burn bridges, but do watch that you aren't wasting your precious communication time, so you don't get burned yourself.

STRATEGY

Don't Worry; Be Happy

Common Sense and Practical Cynicism

It goes without saying that most of us activists are always right—
right? Well, maybe not most, and maybe not always. Sometimes it's
easy to get too caught up in our own good causes to look at things
objectively. But there are basic tenets in the activist's unwritten contract that set us apart from the educrats, for, unlike the Hippocratic
Oath, the Educratic Oath seems to hold no *first cause no harm*
clause.

1. We generally have no ulterior motives behind our activities.
2. Whether we are correct in our beliefs or not, we truly believe
   in what we are doing.
3. Nobody's twisting our arm to do what we do. In fact . . .
4. We've usually had to think long and hard about our cause before we've talked ourselves into taking a stand.

Most of us have a tendency to trust people—even when we may
know better and especially if we are honest ourselves. It isn't always
dishonesty that causes people to fall through on their word or over-
look a problem. Sometimes people forget things and sometimes
they aren't prepared to deal with the truth. If something is important enough to complain about, then it is important enough to

follow up on, after I have complained. Just because my concern is important to me, doesn't mean it is important to the person with the ability to make things right. If you're going to carry a torch, carry it at least until you get to the next runner. Then it will be out of your hands and maybe off your conscience.

One of the few times I went to a principal about a problem with a teacher was when my oldest son was in fourth grade. His teacher found it appropriate to bring a bazaar item—a friend had bought it for her at a bazaar—to class and use it as an object lesson. The only reason I knew about the "dammit doll" was that my older daughter saw my son fashioning something out of matchless socks one day and asked what he was doing. "Making a dammit doll," was his reply. This was a little rag doll meant for hitting and cursing at, to vent frustration.

I had a talk with my son, and he returned the socks to the box on top of the dryer. Even he knew I wouldn't approve, which is why he had been making it in secret. I'm not sure he's ever forgiven his sister for ratting him out.

At the parent/teacher conference a week later, I didn't have to bring up the subject of this sock doll. The teacher began by telling me how much Joseph seemed to enjoy striking the doll and yelling at it. Mind you, Joseph's four-year-old siblings were at home, just waiting for him to transfer this practice to them.

"Well, actually, I was meaning to talk to you about that. I really don't approve of this activity."

She assured me she didn't encourage the children to swear at the doll, while they hit it, though some did. Good Lord, have mercy, there is no common sense left in the world!

"I really don't think this is an appropriate school activity," I said.

She agreed to disagree; I didn't.

The next day, I visited the principal, who was simply flabbergasted and promised to talk to the teacher. However, years later I found out that he had never found the opportunity. For all I know the dammit doll still has a home with a new batch of fourth graders each year—or perhaps it has been moved to the staff lounge so that the fourth-grade teachers have something to hit and swear at when they get the results of the awful WASL. Now there would be an appropriate school activity.

One Way to Their Hearts

Feed them, and they will come. In one all-day Saturday religious ed conference, this was the best advice I gleaned. Does this mean the rest of the conference sucked? No, it's a testament to the worth of food as a tool to win friends and influence people.

Home-baked cinnamon rolls have the same affect on a group of thirty junior high kids as they do on a staff room full of teachers or the boardroom full of administrators or a living room full of neighbors. If they're hot when you bring them in, double your score.

In a former life, I had the ambition to become a caterer. Health codes, that one must have a kitchen separate from the family home, kept me from pursuing that interest past parties and a couple of wedding receptions for friends. But in the process I taught myself the fine art of yeast breads and rolls and baking cookies by the gross rather than the dozen. I also took a commercial scratch-baking course at the local trade school. This taught me a few timesaving tricks to fill huge trays of cookies with a short evening's work.

People are busy and most work very hard. If you want them to pay attention to what you have to say, it helps to let them know you care about them and appreciate their work. The gift of food that you spent time to make yourself can say a lot with a little effort.

Another thing I've taught myself is frosting art. Transfer the quip-tips found in Strategy 6 to the top of a cake or cookies and, voilà, instant humor. Of course, that humor may not be so evident when the district superintendent finds a half sheet-cake on his desk, frosted with forget-me-nots sprouting amongst the sentiment, "Save our kindergarten, please." I understand he shipped it off to be consumed in the break room, right quick. I suspect he didn't bother to read the report I delivered with it, but at least he got a clue that I was serious about the whole thing.

The nice round "No WASL" cake that a friend and I took to our state's accountability commission meeting caught many raised eyebrows, as people couldn't help but notice it next to the coffee pot. But nobody had the guts to cut into the thing. We took it away whole and shared it with a couple of teacher friends who agreed with the message and deserved the cake more.

Margaret Davis, in Texas, had to travel to several grocery stores before she finally found one with an in-store bakery that would allow her to special-order red-slashed "TAAS" cookies. Where there's a will to agitate, there's a way to decorate.

Anything that will make a memory for your cause, your thoughts, or your sincerity is worth the effort. For me, food has always worked well. It breaks the ice to break bread. And I can't remember how many times district officials have asked, "Is this safe to eat?" One must be careful around one's offspring when joking about ingredients, however. Mickey VanDerwerker learned this lesson when her young son asked in the presence of state officials if these were the cookies "with the cat litter in them." Oops!

You will find a choice sampling of my school district's favorite treats in Appendix 1, The Activist's Cookbook. Bon appétit!

No Accounting for the Weather

Once we choose a battle or claim a cause as our own, it pays to think things through and make some guesses about outcomes and possible compromises. Education is not an all-or-nothing world, and most educational concerns are not black or white in any respect. Ask yourself what the ideal outcome would be, and then ask yourself what would make you happy. Then consider that, whether you get what you want or not, there are benefits to speaking for what is right that are not always found in the decision of the board or the teacher or the principal.

Sometimes situations beyond the control of local administration can be the most frustrating of all. In dealing with the issue of overcrowding in my own district, most of the decisions being made were between the lesser of evils, not what was best for children. When I lost a fight to keep our kindergarten classes from being bussed to another elementary school, I gained some respect for the next fight of keeping the district from going to a year-round-school plan. When I suggested changing boundaries to equalize enrollment, the district didn't budge until three years later, when it was someone else's idea, but I did gain a seat on the citizen's advisory committee that worked to change the boundaries in a way that was fair and took the feelings of the community seriously.

The road to educational justice is long and tedious—bring snacks and a magazine and a sense of humor and a forgiving attitude. Leave the self-reproach and the 20/20 hindsight at home. Bring them out when you're ready to rethink strategies. As many of us have told children, at one time or another, "Do your best—that's all anyone can ask of you." That's all you can ask of yourself. If your best isn't good enough this time, stand up, walk out of the legislative office or the courtroom, kick the tire of your car, throw something (nonbreakable), buy yourself an ice cream sundae, and drive home to start again.

Taking stock of the situation, your allies, the changes your struggles have wrought or not wrought, considering the wisdom of carrying on and the chances of success can be a turning point or a stopping point. Pounding your head against a brick wall is painful and often mind-warping.

Benefiting the Doubts

A parent worried about the grading policy of an individual teacher should think about whether this is a battle worth fighting or whether it might be better for the student to handle the situation and the D. A teacher frustrated about having to move down the hall to a different classroom might want to think twice before calling in a union representative. If my son is denied transfer to the high school he'd like to attend, we'll sit down and talk about it before I take it the next step, to the school board. The first question to ask about any situation: Is it worth the fight?

The law of self-preservation dictates that we not be nitpickers or "WOLF!" criers. The laws of self-respect and mutual concern say we should be willing to put up with, ignore, and forgive small inconveniences in a human society.

Everyone makes mistakes. Most of us mean well. If we practice handling small trials and tribulations calmly and patiently, and with the humor they might deserve, we reserve our strength and outrage for the bigger, more difficult tasks.

The same son who was caught fashioning a "dammit doll" in fourth grade had problems sewing a pair of shorts in ninth grade. The day before his sewing project was due for a class that had experienced trouble finding a permanent teacher and was on its third long-term substitute, he brought his project home for help. Rather than tear the rather odd-looking piece of apparel completely apart, we made a trip to Grandma's house, where the sewing machine is always out. Digging through her neatly folded stacks of flannel, we found some appropriate print for pajama shorts and went to work. Step by step we cut and pinned and sewed, together.

The next morning, I took the unfortunate waste of materials and time that were the first pair of "shorts" to the principal's office. I held them up for him—the back was sewn to the back and the front to the front, so they were horseshoe-shaped—and said, "This is Joseph's Home and Family Life project. We have sewn a new pair of shorts and turned it in. We need an A or a 'pass' out of this class." He laughed and agreed.

This time the problem was taken care of immediately. The teacher, whom I never met, gave my son an A, and we moved on. Joseph wore the properly sewn shorts for pajamas for several years.

Look at your glass half-full and be positive about day-to-day experiences. Good or bad, experiences cause growth—some cause a regular growth spurt! We can choose whether we want to grow happily and healthily or make ourselves and everyone around us miserable because there is injustice in the world. Children are a joy to work with, if we think they are—so are most adults.

The reputation of an activist is built on battles chosen, company kept, and the ability to act sensibly under pressure. I'm not suggesting that we be quiet and well-behaved by any means, just that we exercise a certain level of care and wisdom in our petitioning and ranting. Discretion will secure a label of "caring advocate"—which opens doors, rather than "chronic whiner"—which, more often than not, gets them slammed in our faces.

"A cheerful activist is an effective activist." Silly as it may sound, repeat that line in your head until you embrace it as your own. If you begin to label every activity of the "enemy" as "corruption," you will lose your ability to go on in the most effective manner. Remembering that everyone is not out to get you or your child or your school, and that it is often insecurity, lack of knowledge, or time restraints that cause the apathy you may see around you, provides the strength to continue to seek allies. If one good woman or man can be found, don't destroy the city. Never allow Don Quixote symptoms to manifest themselves into full-blown cynicism.

I often take my children along to events and meetings—keeps me from forgetting what I came for—and I encourage them to take part and present, when appropriate. As a matter of fact, I've bribed them to present, on occasion. I promised to buy my twins snow-boards, if they would read *Testing Miss Malarkey,* by Judy Finchler, aloud to our state's Academic Achievement and Accountability Commission, at their monthly meeting.

At the February meeting, Carmen and Sam combined their three-minute comment time limits to read the book, sitting bravely at the table with the microphone in front of the panel. (Unfortunately that particular meeting wasn't being recorded for the state's TV broadcast.) Samuel did the reading. A few smiles broke on the faces of the commissioners, but the commission chairperson was not amused.

As Carmen and Samuel returned to their seats in the audience, the chairperson found it appropriate to announce, "Juanita is running for state superintendent and is using her children to campaign for her."

When it was my turn to speak, I sat at the microphone calmly, looked at him, and said, "Mr. Patrick, I am not using my children to campaign for me. My children are the reason I'm campaigning!" The point was well taken by the entire commission, and I continued to present the packet I had brought for them. Never let the rudeness or inappropriateness of others deter you from your mission. Be comfortable with what you are doing and you will be the one who deserves to smile as you leave the room.

On the way home from the meeting, we stopped and bought two $10 snowboards at Kmart. Friday of that week, it snowed, which it rarely does in the Puget Sound area of Western Washington. Carmen and Sam got their reward!

When protesting on a corner, cheerfully greet the people walking by. You are the host of the show. Act the part. When presenting to a board, act pleasantly professional while you demonstrate with facts and figures that they've just made the dumbest decision you've ever seen in your life. When you're down and out of ideas, give yourself a break until you feel better about the world and your place in it. If you're feeling out of place amidst "the suits," order yourself a gold nameplate that says, "Agitative Consultant." When all else fails, remember you'd rather be one of *us* than one of *them.* Whoever your *us* and *them* are.

Dish It Out With a Small, Sterling Spoon

Little Pictures

The color red is utilized in fast-food and other advertisements for a reason. Children respond to bright colors, and the color red stimulates hunger. All we have to do now is figure out what color stimulates intelligent thought in adults, and educational activists will have it made!

Christmas 2000 brought me perhaps the most useful gift I've ever received, a semiautomatic, Badge-a-Minit, tabletop button-maker. By its one-year anniversary, I had spread 14,000 little pictures and punchy slogans throughout the nation. I had wanted the machine to prepare for my campaign to become state superintendent. The networking that the de-testing buttons have brought about is pure serendipity!

Perhaps my favorite button story belongs to Arizona activist Gabie Gedlaman, who requested that I make a button for her son. Gabie pinned the message on her seventeen-month-old son Ruben's stroller, when she took him along to an education meeting at the state capitol. The associate state superintendent was admiring the little boy and began reading the button aloud: "My mom fights standardized test abuse." The next words out of her mouth were, "Oh, my!" as she stopped reading before she got to "How about yours?"

My buttons have been noticed on tables in teachers' lounges and on union leaders at national conventions. They have been pictured in activist newspapers, single-page handouts and overheads, and *The School Administrator* magazine of the American Association of School Administrators. Buttons are magic! And the contact information, printed on a return address sticker on the back, makes them as good as any business card. Around the country, certain designs have become favorites and I receive a constant stream of email requests and comments.

From California:

Hello,
I need 50 more buttons of the "Test-Teach" variety. I gave one to a couple of our district's top administrators and now all of our principals want them.

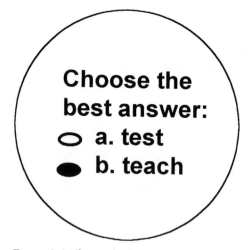

Figure 6–1 Choose the Best Answer

From New York:

The buttons are great. In NYC I brought a bunch. The Proud Parent of (Bar Code) was a real hit. One guy looked at me and laughed and said, "Oooh, that is dark!" Yeah!

Figure 6–2 Proud Parent of Bar Code

From Utah:
I have a fellow assistant principal that attended the Improving America's Schools conference last week. She received a button that stated "Every Child Tested." I am doing a presentation on accountability and would love to have a couple of your buttons for our group presenting.

Figure 6–3 No Child Left Untested

Activism is communication. We live in a fast-paced, catch-phrase society that is addicted to entertainment. If our message is presented in an easy-access, punch-line fashion, we might just be able to get a small point made, in the two-second attention span of the average American adult.

In my button campaign, I've found that the most successful graphic is the red slash, universal symbol for "NO!" I think most of us walk around on the edge of agitation most days, whether we are activists or not, so we are naturally drawn to find out what someone else dislikes about the world, just in case they might be in agreement with what we dislike about the world.

Bugs displayed behind the slash were popular for a while, mostly as an ad for exterminator companies. No "Whining" has worn out its cuteness. But as I wore my red-slashed testing acronym through the crowds at our local fair this year, I watched the nods and smiles. Then, as I walked past a bench, someone pointed and yelled, "Yah!" motioning me to her. She grabbed and shook my hand as she said, "I'm a teacher. I moved out of fourth grade because of the WASL and now do you know what they're doing to fifth grade?! The science WASL!" I left her with a few buttons, my activist card, and the knowledge that I was running for state superintendent in 2004. She pledged her vote.

Wearing my "No Apathy" button to events at my kids' junior high, I've been asked by students several times, "What's 'apathy'?" Ah, the teachable moment!

State Senator Harold Hochstatter ordered 200 red-slashed "WASL" buttons to give to visitors to the capitol and high school pages working for the state legislators. Zach is a sixth grader whose mom works at the state capitol. Zach's mom gave him a button she got from the senator, and Zach emailed me asking if I could send him two dozen buttons for his homeroom class at Reeves Middle School in Olympia. I sent the buttons to him right away, and he responded that the kids were all asking for buttons and they offered to pay for them, but he just gave them away for free. His teachers were even wearing them. He wanted to know if I could send him 200 more.

I put 100 buttons and a "No WASL" shirt in the mail to Zach the next day. Then I began hearing from Zach's classmates. One boy wanted fifty-three buttons for a friend who went to another school.

Figure 6–4 Red-slashed Testing Acronyms

Another student asked for twenty buttons. Some students were emailing me from computers at school. Apparently, the kids at Reeves Middle School don't know what apathy is either.

I heard from two moms who had received buttons from Senator Hochstatter. One was forming a nonprofit to fight for school improvement and against WASL. The other wanted buttons to hand out at a school meeting. She has since depleted the first 100 and asked for 100 more.

It is indeed a small educational world. My pharmacist asked about my "Parent Our Schools" button one day while she was ringing up my prescriptions. I told her a little about my campaign against high-stakes testing and for the position of state superintendent. She gave me the name of her brother-in-law, who is an Education Service District Superintendent. An ESD is a regional center

Figure 6–5 Parent Our Schools

that oversees several local school districts. I wasn't aware that they had superintendents until my pharmacist told me she's related to one. Virtually everyone is related to a teacher or administrator or a PTA president. Wearing your activism on your shirt will bring out the best in educational relations.

Heightened airport security proved helpful to the cause recently, as the security man who was checking me over with a metal detecting wand noticed my "Choose the best answer" button and commented that it was a good one. "You want it?"

"Sure, I collect buttons."

"I'm fighting high-stakes testing nationwide," I said, "My goal is 10,000 buttons for the year."

"That's good!"

"My email and website are on the back."

"I'll check that out." My metal scan completed, he cleared me to pick up my carry-ons, and I proceeded to the gate.

Graphic support software, a good printer, and a little imagination go a long way. Original thought processes help, but they're not a necessity. Just look around and see what advertising schemes seem to work. Tug and twist at district, state, or national propaganda photos, pictures from soft drink commercials or the war on drugs—"YOUR BRAIN on high-stakes testing."

Make the slogan fit the occasion. When I learned that the Seattle School District is jumping ahead of the state and requiring the class of 2004 to take the tenth grade WASL in order to graduate, I had to switch gears from telling parents to opt their tenth graders out of the test. The new button is, "You can test me, but you can't make me score!" Civil disobedience is the only option for students who want their diploma but disagree with the test. There may be a lot of protest essays on the writing test answer-sheets in Seattle.

Sound Bites Out of Crime

We've been told pictures are worth a thousand words since we were old enough to carry on a conversation, but carefully chosen words can stick in the craw, or the mind, of a public official for a long, long time—particularly if positioned properly in the press or on buttons spread throughout the service area or on an overhead or the front of a report presented in public. Every now and then, a message gets back to me from some distant area of the state or country about some slogan I put on a button or sticker or shirt. "We don't say 'WASL SCHMASL,' here!" The statement was made by an assistant principal during a start of the year teachers' meeting. Makes me wonder who gave her the offending button. Anyway, she's mistaken, because they now say, "WASL SCHMASL" quite often all over the state. I've probably made 2,000 buttons that say it. And her district

Figure 6–6 WASL SCHMASL!

was an area for targeted assistance. As we say in email-land, "Laugh Out Loud!"

Make your educational goal part of your life, and the opportunities to win friends and influence people suddenly become endless. When I travel, I wear a T-shirt or sweatshirt with some sort of educational message on the front and back. This way, when I'm waiting in a line I'm educating people behind me, and when I'm walking down long airport corridors or riding those walking sidewalks, I'm getting looks of agreement, amusement, disgust, or puzzlement from everyone I pass. The response to the big red lips design of the Texas testing resistance is particularly amusing. And as I boarded a plane, wearing my "Flag the Tests" pledge, the man behind me said, "So, you don't like algebra, huh?" The opportunity for enlightenment strikes—again and again.

I've burned out two irons on the transfers I order by the hundreds from <www.hanes2U.com>. Computer printable transfers are now available for light and dark material and can be found at most discount and office supply stores.

Figure 6–7 Read My Lips

WE PLEDGE ALLEGIANCE TO THE TEST

AND TO THE STANDARDS FOR WHICH IT STANDS

ONE NATION UNDER THE FORTUNE 500

AND ALGEBRA FOR ALL

WITH HIGH STAKES

RAISING CHILDREN OF THE GLOBAL ECONOMY

BY THE GLOBAL ECONOMY AND FOR THE GLOBAL ECONOMY

WITH ACCOUNTABILITY AND PRODUCTIVITY FOR ALL

Figure 6–8 Flag the Tests is a joint project with fellow test-resisters/email buddies Susan Ohanian and Gloria Pipkin. Susan wrote the stripes, Gloria gathered the stars and I sewed them together in a graphic for note cards, shirts, mugs, bags, and anything else that can be ironed on or printed. Some items can be ordered from Café Press <www.cafepress.com/FlagtheTests>. Any profits from this project go to George Schmidt and Substance. Betsy Ross would be proud!

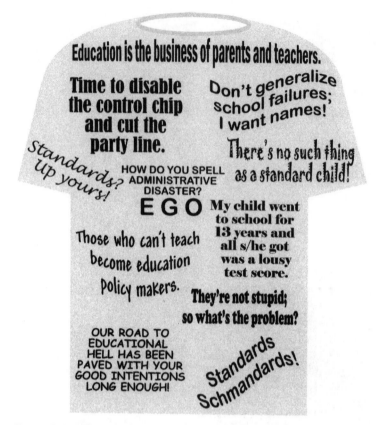

Figure 6–9 T-Shirt Wisdom and Winning One-Liners

It can keep an activist grinning inwardly for days to have played the right flashcard phrase at the right moment—a quip, a jab, something shocking that they don't expect to see in print or hear from your mouth. I have to admit there is no education official in the state of Washington who is surprised at anything that I write or say anymore, but the jabs are still just as potent in the minutes of an accountability meeting or in the press or at a public hearing.

Sum it up in ten words or less. Print it in bold type. Deliver it with a smile. Roll the dice and take your turn when your name is read from the sign-in sheet. Good thoughts come in short sentences.

I'm So Confused!

Those in positions of power are apt to utilize any kind of response they think will lull you into accepting their decisions. One ploy that is often used is to tell you they have never heard the complaint you are voicing from any other source. "That's funny, Mr. Whiner, we haven't gotten any other negative feedback about the new four-hour PE classes." Another trick is to play dumb and attempt to wear down your resistance with lines such as, "Help me to understand." School-smart activists can easily turn these tired tactics against offensive officials.

When faced with confused deer-in-the-headlights, step on the gas and run them down with information or spell it out for them

---

Fluff (as defined by Juanita Doyon as it applies to our school district for the week of May 7, 2000)

1. Any unproven educational reform measure
2. Any item that detracts from the first order of business for the year and month—bond passage
3. Any item that is given priority over basic student welfare and safety during a time when schools are overcrowded and staff is overextended
4. Wassie the Whale (visit Wassie at *www.wassiethewhale.com*)
5. State-mandated, unproven testing methods that detract from routine learning time and harm children with unrealistic expectations
6. New textbooks that contain incorrect information and are useless for basic education and thus useless for advanced, applied learning
7. WASL academies (unless they are renamed and refocused to bypass the concept of "teaching to the test")
8. The use of educational jargon
9. Lack of recognition of the need to meet the public on their terms
10. The encouragement of teaching methods that are so untraditional that they leave parents out of the educational loop

---

Figure 6–10

with the childlike simplicity they seem to need. What would I say to a child in kindergarten? Begin at the beginning. List the troubles you see and your reasons for disagreement. Provide them workable alternatives. Use a form that suits the occasion. Draw them a picture, if necessary. Write them a poem to keep their short attention spans in check. I learned that my district superintendent hated petitions, so I utilized them at every opportunity. If you get them to display anger, while you are displaying utmost calm and coolheaded reasoning, you have them where you want them.

When asked to define a term I used in an email to describe the outlook of our district superintendent, I simply handed a school board member an envelope containing the page shown in Figure 6–10, at the next board meeting. It was adorned with a pretty little blue feather.

Waste Not, Want Not: Seize the Moment, the Idea, and the Half-price Printer Supplies

There is a certain joy that comes from thinking about the hierarchy of the Educational Government and all the political clout, corporate cronies, and millions and billions of dollars at their command, and then considering what a dent can be made in that power when a few teachers and parents get together, make a few poster-board signs, and stand on a corner waving to drivers and greeting those walking by on their way to or from work. There is more joy when school buses drive by while you're holding your "HONK IF YOU'RE TIRED OF TAAS" (Texas Assessment of Academic Standards) signs, and honk, circle the block, and honk again. There is still more joy when your protest is held outside a convention center where the national education secretary is scheduled to speak, and the news cameras are rolling while a class of third graders marches by reading your protest signs, yelling, "Honk, honk, honk, honk . . ." all the way into the national convention where they will perform for the attendees.

Working in our spare time, it becomes important to keep things simple and easy, latching onto anything that works well the first time, repeating it, and sharing the strategy with others whenever possible. Here, I'm learning as I go, and often need to pay more

Figure 7–1 Nevada Test Site

attention to my own advice. The wonder of the last year or so has been the ease with which I've found new contacts and made new friends. In every level of education, people are yearning for common sense, understanding, and hope. They are hungry for our message!

The Improving America's Schools Conference is an annual affair put on by the U.S. Department of Education in three locations around the nation. When friends and I dropped in on the fall 2001 versions of the conference in Reno, Nevada, and San Antonio, Texas, we found hundreds of allies among the teachers, administrators, and parents attending the conferences. Our bright spots of dissent, amidst the education department propaganda, were a welcome sight as people came from sessions that told them child-centered education is a myth, that few schools are using federal funds successfully, and that the only way schools will improve is with federally mandated testing.

In Reno, Michelle Trusty-Murphy and I wandered the conference venue handing out 500 de-testing buttons in two days. Michelle led me by example in a hands-on crash course in *Working a Room!* "Good morning. We're giving away buttons today. Would you like some?"

This of course led many times to a conversation about who we were and why we were there. "We are the resistance!"

The next month, I traveled to San Antonio, where I met up with several members of the Texas test-resistance. Because of the cordial response that Michelle and I received at the Reno conference, I was positive that we would have a good time and find allies in San Antonio. When we arrived at the huge Henry B. Gonzalez Convention Center, we followed the directions of the high school greeters upstairs to the vendor area. We had not registered as conference participants, so we had no name badges to attend conference sessions. We were delighted to find an empty booth, where we stood for a little while, talking to anyone who walked by.

As the reception to our information seemed warm, we soon found ourselves sitting behind the table, with our buttons and information spread before us. All day we sat there, handing out our wares. When we arrived late the second day, people were looking for us, telling us we were the best part of the conference. Several people came by multiple times, laughing to see that we hadn't been removed. We saw that it was good, and on the third day we protested on the street corner, the one with the school buses and children going by as if we had placed a special order for them.

Wise Buys

As I've stepped up to the banquet-sized protest plate, I've spent hundreds of hours brainstorming and getting in touch with the little voice in my head—the one that wakes me up with a really good button slogan at 2 A.M. I've also switched from hunting down craft bargains for the kindergarten class to checking out the markdown table at Office Depot. My dining room is now full of really cheap envelopes for computer-generated cards. The envelopes make a nice accompaniment to the reams of card stock I found last year on the same table for 88¢ each.

Activism on a shoestring is a challenge, but my personal beliefs tell me that God is on our side, and His eye is on not only the sparrow, but also on us loudmouth magpies spreading the good word of educational improvement. He will provide! What other explanation could there be for finding cheap ink for my printer when I need it and address labels in the really big boxes for $5? It's loaves and fishes all over again. Ask and ye shall receive a rebate; seek and ye shall find a bargain!

Many of us parents and teachers have done the PTA or PTO thing for years. That respectable experience means we already know how to run a fundraiser, make posters, write proposals for donations, and put up signs on grocery store bulletin boards. Just remember, it's the little things that add up to the big things and throw a wrench into the well-oiled machine of big business and big government or smear the rubber stamp of the state or local school board.

Quick-tips, Time-savers, and Lessons-learned

Save and print as you go. After about a year of collecting names, emails, and comments from around the state and nation, I had been religiously saving them to a computer file and planning to print out all the "first contact" emails. My poor husband felt just awful when he accidentally dumped my saved mail and my most current address book while rebooting the computer. I didn't yell—it was more my fault than his, because I had practiced printing procrastination. Fortunately, most of my email addresses were retrievable, as I had saved them on a disc.

Know who, what, and where you are and call in the press. When Mary Obrien, the Ohio coordinator for the Assessment Reform Network, arrived to stay at my house the week of the American Education Research Association conference, she immediately asked for the phone book. In it she found the local television and newspaper numbers and started dialing. Her side of the conversation was going something like this, as I listened in awe: Hello, could you connect me with the person I would talk to about news stories? Yes, this is Mary Obrien. I am the volunteer coordinator for Assessment Reform Network, from Ohio, and I will be presenting at the American Education Research Association Conference this week, on the subject of high-stakes testing. Yes, like your state's WASL test. We are opposed to the testing and will be holding a panel discussion. I'm staying at the home of Juanita Doyon, who is the Washington coordinator for Assessment Reform Network. I thought you would probably like to have a person covering the story for your station/paper. We will be at the Seattle Convention Center, presenting a panel discussion on test resistance tomorrow at 10:00 A.M. I can be reached at 253/846–0823. Thank you.

Duplicate the good stuff. Loving to write letters and emails, I have personally answered dozens of first contact emails personally and completely, telling about my background, my activism activities, etc. This can take a half hour or more for each new contact. Since I have been writing articles and a book, I find it difficult to tell every contact everything I want to in the first email, so I've decided it would be okay to make a "form" introduction email. This can be personalized easily, by writing a two-line introduction. It gets my contact information and background quickly into the hands of the contact and it's just as effective as writing out the same information new each time I'm contacted. People always write back, and then I can respond in more detail to whatever has drawn their interest in my first post.

Play cards and carry a score pad. A business card is a wonderful tool. Activist cards are even better. If you're making contact with people in your community or beyond, it is very handy to hand them a preprinted card with all your contact information on it. My card also has a philosophy statement on the back and a catchy graphic. I try to remember to carry a small notebook for writing down the contact information of others. This is a concept, like "Save it and print it NOW!" that I must work a little harder on myself.

Don't hide out. Not every activist is trying to reach hoards of people. But I am. Consequently, I have my name, email address, phone, and website listed on just about everything I hand out or every piece of writing I submit to individuals or to newspapers. People find me. I am accessible. Worried moms call in the middle of the day. High school kids email late at night. Reporters leave messages on my answering machine. Fellow activists who are also friends have my cell phone number. My home number is listed in the book. I answer emails promptly; I call people back; I follow through. Accessibility is a personal thing, and each of us needs to figure out just how much time we have to commit to communicating. But consider carefully, if you want to grow a movement, it is not the time to hide under a bushel.

Pick a spot and picket. The right to picket is something everyone should experience first-hand—and it doesn't have to be a protest outside The Gap, being cranky at prospective shoppers at Christmastime. It only takes three or four people—and some of them can be little people; activists in training—to present a respectable protest on a busy street corner at rush hour.

Juanita Doyon
20421 4th Ave E
Spanaway, WA 98387
253/846-0823
Jedoyon@aol.com
www.rereformed.com
WA Coordinator for Assessment Reform Network,
In association with *www.FairTest.org*
Coordinator, Mother Against WASL
Candidate, WA Superintendent of Public Instruction

> The only viable alternative to data collection is human engagement.

Figure 7–2 Activist Card

Make a few posters. Most home publishing programs have a poster or sign option, which will print out a nice big piece together protest prop, or if you prefer permanent markers directly on poster board, that works too. My friends and I used poster board, computer-made pictures, and glue-sticks and then cover the finished poster with clear Con-Tact paper to protect it from weather and keep it in good shape for several events. Be sure to take along information sheets and other handouts. A corner with an easily accessible parking lot, such as a gas station or convenience store, allows people to stop and talk and pick up buttons, information, and opt-out forms.

Make it official. Doug Selwyn, David Marshak, and Robert Howard are three college professors who got together and wrote Initiative Number 780 to the People of Washington State. In Washington, citizens can write ballot initiatives, collect signatures, and get them put to a vote of the people.

So the professors are running a campaign to collect the required 200,000 signatures. If they do—with a lot of help from their friends—the people will vote on a law that states, in part: "Every candidate must complete all sections of the 10th Grade WASL before filing a declaration and affidavit of candidacy and must list all of his or her scores accurately on the standard form. Any falsehood listed on the declaration and affidavit of candidacy in relation to the WASL scores shall be subject to prosecution under penalty of perjury. The Secretary of State shall list all candidates' WASL scores both on a web site established for this purpose and in every edition of the Voters' Pamphlet."

Pure genius! Because the initiative doesn't call to do away with WASL, teachers and administrators feel free to sign it. Because it puts our elected officials to the test—literally—just about everybody is willing to sign. And the true beauty of the plan is that even if 200,000 signatures aren't collected, at least many, many discussions will be had about the WASL and why we don't agree with it for our kids. I like to think of the initiative as a golden ruling: Test others as you would have them test you.

Free-flowing Speech

When I was in high school, my choir teacher gave each choir member a copy of a *Reader's Digest* article entitled, "How Will They Know Unless I Tell Them?" It was years before I actually read the article, which I stashed away with my other high school memorabilia. It was something about a teenager telling her parents that she loved them or some such homey drivel. As a parent, I know good and well that my teenagers love me, but that they would never say it unless they were dying or miles away at a summer job they hate or both. Okay, so we're just *that* kind of a family. But the title of the article pops into my head daily as I go about my life as a full-time activist.

What if I don't get up in front of the board and tell them what I know? Things that are obvious to me might not be obvious to the principal. The state superintendent might not have time to talk to parents about what they want for their kids. I better get these thoughts on paper, through my massive email list, or on the air. I better give them no excuse to say nobody told them so. I better teach these head-in-the-sand egotists a thing or two about investigative reporting! A missed opportunity to communicate is, well, a missed opportunity to communicate.

Margaret Davis and Carol Holst, along with a few others in their town of Alvin, Texas, dubbed themselves the "gabby moms" when they began fighting standardized dress and standardized tests. They are known to attend school board meetings wearing ropes around their waists to protest the silly and degrading practice of school officials making students wear the same, if they forget to wear a belt to school. Student inspections, when students are asked to line up in the hall to be checked for dress code violations, have become a regular occurrence.

Taking the standardized dress policy to the limit, the Alvin School Board denies parent requests for waivers, even though the policy itself used to state that philosophical and religious objections would be honored. The board decided to remove the word *philosophical*, presumably because Margaret was using it to fight for what she believes is her right to dress her children as she sees fit. Margaret recently decided to run for school board herself and wonders what to tackle first: dress standards, test standards, or denominational prayer at public school board meetings standards.

Whatever the front burner topic of choice, Carol and Margaret have come up with an idea to get people of their town talking. They decided to get out the soapbox. Margaret's husband, Charlie, built a box big enough to stand on, and the women take it to the town's public park each Sunday afternoon. Now, every email from Carol or Margaret is signed "See you at the soapbox." They have had a nice article in the *Houston Chronicle,* and there are growing numbers of people attending and speaking each week. On a first come/first speak basis, participants are free to speak on any issue. Simple, cheap, popular, and fun—the perfect activism activity.

For Successful Presentations

1. **Write it down.** Even if you are presenting beauty contestant style, in an evening gown, there will always be one judge who is better at reading than he is at listening. Always present a packet of information or a sheet of talking points for later perusal. If you are presenting to a panel or board and there is an audience, be sure to provide the audience with copies. One never quite knows what allies lurk in the masses. From experience: At the break in any meeting, walk around and visit the restroom for additional networking opportunities. Be sure you have your materials with you.
2. **Speak slowly and loudly.** Rehearsal is the best bet, here. We are not all natural born orators. I am more of a shrinking-

violet—well, I used to be. Practice can make for near perfection.

3. **Use props.** And use them to your best advantage. If an overhead is available, come prepared to use it. If you know a favorite analogy of your adversaries, turn it against them by making it real. I once clunked a hammer down in front of the state superintendent, who is fond of comparing testing with this carpentry essential.

   Appropriate cartoons on the overhead can win the day. Catch 'em off-guard with some well-placed humor. If you're good with rhythm and rhyme, use that against them with satirical poetry. Boards and panels are accustomed to those who sign in to speak being a little on the underprepared side. Fancy presentation materials usually come out only with district committees reporting on newly adopted math or reading programs. Dazzle them with your footwork!

4. **Watch the clock.** Anything worth saying to a board can be said very carefully in one minute or less. Anything beyond that should be supporting facts, data, and opinion. Many opportunities for public input limit each speaker, sometimes to as little as one or two minutes. Whereas five minutes can seem like an eternity, three minutes speed by fast. Practice with an egg timer. Better yet, take the egg timer with you and start it with your presentation. Never underestimate the willingness of an irritated official to count grains of sand and cut you off mid-sentence and mid-important-point.

5. **Read it, if you must.** When I really have to keep things within a time frame, and there are very specific thoughts I have to get across, I write it out word for word and read it. This works best for me, when what I want to say is particularly pointed or necessarily nasty. If I'm telling the state super she doesn't know good educational administrative practice from a hole in the ground, it's best not to rely on my short-term memory and on-the-spot composure.

6. **Stare them in the eye.** I usually give the people I'm talking to a copy of what I'm presenting before I present it. Even during my first presentations, when I was extremely nervous, I enjoyed watching the facial expression of those reading ahead, who were thinking, "She's going to say what?!" Then I

would deliver the sentences to the whole room. Look them in the face and make them know you mean what you're saying.

7. **Be polite.** Occasional fist-pounding aside, I always do my best to say it with a smile, thank them for allowing me to speak, and act as though they have my respect, deserved or not. My Daddy always taught me that you can win more flies with honey. Having regard for your surroundings is very important, if you ever want to be respected for your opinion. Remember the raving lunatic—respect is a two-way street.

8. **Don't spare the tears, but use them sparingly.** Emotional pleas have their place. There are many ways to wrench the guts of those to whom you're presenting. Once, when I was the token parent on a board presentation team, I took the 8×10 glossy of my seventh-grade son, "just to prove I am a parent." My very effective overhead for this plea to maintain the school's Seventh Grade Academy was:

> Everything I need to know about life, I learned from my seventh grader. Acceptance is Cool. Chips and dips are a major food group. If you must follow the rules, act like you wrote them. Act your age only when absolutely necessary. When all else fails—sleep in. Family is alright, but friends are better. Dress casual. Emotions are best worn on your sleeve. Homework is something you do on the bus. We could all use a year to adjust.

Several days after the presentation, two teachers at the junior high asked for permission to use this *everything* list with their classes. Never hesitate to demonstrate your own emotional attachments to appeal to the empathy of others. Then, even if they don't do what you want, they may at least feel guilty about it.

STRATEGY
8   Appeal and Appeal to the Press

S ome of the more interesting and challenging aspects of the past few months have been brought about by my conversion to *media princess* (written with a smirk!). The limelight is not a place I ever in my wildest imagination pictured myself. Writing has always been my thing, and I have never been a natural presenter. That is changing, rapidly.

With the release of a front-page article in our local paper, picturing my son and me in our official no-WASL wear, a wave of publicity hit my family. Associated Press picked up the article during testing week. One television station called that day and all other local stations called the next morning, beginning at 6:00 A.M. Two stations came to our home for interviews and the others interviewed my two youngest children and me in front of the junior high school.

The school district's communications person became involved to handle the press and keep them from interfering with the school day. Radio stations began calling for interviews. Other newspapers caught on and wanted quotes for their own local stories. I quickly discovered that, yes, I really could think on my feet. I got out my protest posters for background in the living room shots, prayed that my short-term memory would stay by me while the camera was rolling, and enjoyed my five minutes of fame, which is exactly the amount of time the taped news broadcasts from every channel came to—five minutes.

Each form of mass media has unique characteristics and a variety of opportunities for exposure. The trick is to use free publicity to your best advantage and enjoy the experience. Stretching out your time in the spotlight is the only way to profit from the press.

Newsprint and Magazines

Easiest, cheapest, and most forgiving, newspapers can offer great opportunities for editorial comment. We Americans worship our children—we don't always *do* what's best for them, but we do for the most part *want* what's best for them and value youth. So, anything to do with our future adult citizens, including education, can be big news. The easiest way to begin to use newspapers is to write letters to the editor.

Scan your local paper's editorial or letters page for rules and submission suggestions or get online and search for papers state- or nationwide. Larger metropolitan papers usually accept submissions from a wider service-area than small local papers or weeklies. Most have their guidelines on their websites and accept email submissions. Honing the 200-word essay is the key to frequent publication of letters. If you are an enthusiastic writer and can write an interesting piece of 600 words or so, look for the op-ed or guest editorial section as a place to voice your concerns. Use whatever titles you hold, if this seems appropriate. Papers often feature education professionals as local experts. Watch the opinion pages to see what gets printed and aim your submissions accordingly.

The other way to get into print is to contact reporters. Good reporters like controversy and are happy to cover both sides of an issue, even if yours is not the popular side. Read bylines or find the education reporters in the contact lists of the newspaper. Many articles have a contact phone number and email at the bottom, requesting input. Once reporters know you as a willing contact, you may be called whenever the subject you are working with comes up in the news. Quotes make a story, so make yourself quotable and you will be more likely to get help to get your message out.

Magazines and education journals are often interested in subjects of controversy. Their regular writers actively seek attitudes of parents, teachers, and all others involved in education. Keep an eye on mainstream publications, such as *Family Circle, Newsweek,* and *Ladies Home Journal*—all of which have featured articles on high-stakes testing in the past year—and the professional publications, such as *Journal of Curriculum and Supervision,* published by the Association for Supervision and Curriculum Development, or *English Leadership Quarterly,* published by National Council of Teachers of English, which can be accessed on the Internet through association websites. Most magazines feature reader feedback space, which can be a good forum for your comments. Some offer online opinion boards and reader polls. Some journals require membership or paid subscription to access; some don't.

On Air

Radio is a fascinating medium and perhaps the most political of all mass media. Radio offers many opportunities to air your opinions and your plans for action as well as solicit allies. Radio stations have a lot of airtime to fill, and it can't possibly all be sold as commercial time or played up in songs. Listen to your local stations, AM and FM, and figure out who to call. Listen to national affiliates and find out where education fits into their scheduling.

Many stations actively solicit for listener-generated discussion topics and will allow you to advertise events for free. Call-in shows often feature education topics. There are pitfalls to the politics and open debate, however. You cannot edit your own phone call, and you are not in control of the host of the segment.

There are many radio hosts who thrive on making callers sound like zealots. Be prepared to remain calm. Write out your notes well and become familiar with the host's style before calling in. A professional talker can back even the most experienced conference presenter into a corner. Also, be prepared to field questions and disagreement from other callers or opposing experts.

It sometimes helps to email or phone the host and explain your subject in detail before attempting to argue for it on the air. This can give the host a better perspective and win them to your point beforehand. I once called in to argue against—you guessed it—our state testing. The host was bashing teachers and doing his best to discount everything I said—even though I had established that I wasn't a teacher myself. I got cut off, so my son called in—and got cut off even quicker.

Then my husband emailed the host and explained what I was trying to say. The host contacted him and asked if he would be on the show on a different day. My husband got to make the points I was trying to make, with a little more time, and the host had become much more reasonable, embracing what my husband said as enlightenment, rather than argument. Wonders never cease, my husband does know what I'm talking about and can argue it just as well or better than I can! Hmm.

This same radio host asked me to be a guest again during the next season of testing. This time, I was prepared for his style of guest-badgering. He discounted my twenty-two years of parenting. He attempted to bring my religion into the picture, as if that would automatically mark me a fanatic. He tried to portray my cause as a tiny faction. I held my own, remained calm, and, at the end of the conversation, told him that I have nearly 300 people on my email list, that the Assessment Reform Network has coordinators in thirty-seven states, that I hoped he had learned something, and that I hoped he would read my book. He said to send it and he would. I will—and just maybe he'll learn something more.

The Tube

I had been practicing my generally slothful in-and-out-and-dump-and-go housekeeping all week, when the TV station called wanting a statement on the year's test score release. "Would it be okay to send the cameraman out in about half an hour?"

"Uh, would it be alright if they shot OUTSIDE?" I led the cameraman to the garage, where I had assembled my protesting supplies in my car trunk, ready to take to the release of the scores the next day. Television crews are more than willing to work with you. They want their shots. They may tape for half an hour and use only ten seconds, but that's show business. Television news is, after all, television. And don't you forget it. Give them what they want—a good story. Make it poignant for the viewing audience. Tell them something they need to know. Think of five points you'd like to get across.

If you find the phone ringing off the hook from every station in town, concentrate on a different point for each station. For example, my complaints about WASL include the guinea pig use of my children (Channel 4), the cost (Channel 5), the waste of instruction time (Channel 7). When Channel 13 came to the house, I had already interviewed with the other three stations. The reporter wanted a new slant and discussed this with me before taping. So I told him I was running for office and that I was fighting the *educrats*. He liked it! It was the best coverage I received.

Work with reporters and treat them as friends. They are in the people business and most are extremely kind and friendly. Be honest and sincere and your story will come through, even if it is in small increments.

Finding comfort in front of the camera is something that requires forethought and in some cases a lot of self-talk—"I can do this; I can do this!" I tend to think of it as an out-of-body experience, but it has been easier and feels more natural than I could have imagined.

Not all of us will get to the point where we depend on mass publicity for our cause, but if your fight reaches this rather bizarre level, enjoy it! Don't be afraid to watch and tape yourself. If it becomes a habit, learn as you go. Real people telling the truth are what our schools need more than anything. The general public is sick to death of political hogwash.

Beyond the news hour, many stations have local talk shows. There are also local access cable stations, some owned by colleges, who may be willing to tape or air a live debate or information segment. I have taken part in two talk shows in the past year, one on local public television and one on a local access station. If you are handed publicity on a silver platter, be gracious as you accept it and take a bow when your point is well made.

STRATEGY

9

Learn From the Masters, But Think for Yourself

To Boldly Go Where No Mom Has Gone Before

If you don't know a Libertarian from a librarian, a quick study of political direction and players may be in order. Think of a game of Monopoly, and you get the gist of how things work in the world of political activism. There will always be those who just have to get their choice of the markers first. Big brother insists on being the banker. Some participants want to buy up all the property and always seem to have just a little more cash available than anyone else. Storming off when the game gets hard or drags on too long is a popular choice, as is refusing to play, if we have consistently lost in the past.

Locally or nationally, I often find myself standing in the middle of the Reading Railroad tracks waiting for the next train to come barreling down on me from either side. Unfortunately, nobody ever seems to want to pay that $200 rent for landing in my space!

Education is a politically polarizing topic. Nevertheless, regular folks can find points of agreement, if we look and listen. Yes, this can be tricky, because government and educationists themselves have corrupted education language so thoroughly that the *right* insists the *left* holds the government ear and the *left* insists the *right* does. And sometimes those of us in the middle just don't feel we can get along with anybody.

The first important step to finding common ground is to find one thing that we agree on. Set all teaching methods and curriculum—which tend to be some of the hottest, yet often least important, buttons—aside for a moment and ask some basic questions.

- What purpose does public education serve?
- Who is responsible for the education of a child?
- How can money be more wisely spent?
- What are the problems and/or needs of the local school?

The answers may be varied and broad, but they can be a starting place for discussion. Discussion is good. It means people are at least interested.

In my own state, I work with Puget Sound Rethinking Schools—a group associated with the national Rethinking Schools organization. Some call the opening from <www.rethinkingschools .org> a statement of *liberal principle:*

> Schools are about more than producing efficient workers or future winners of the Nobel Prize for science. They are the place in this society where children from a variety of backgrounds come together and, at least in theory, learn to talk, play, and work together.
>
> Schools are integral not only to preparing all children to be full participants in society, but also to be full participants in this country's ever-tenuous experiment in democracy. That this vision has yet to be fully realized does not mean it should be abandoned.

Forget *liberals* or *conservatives*. These are good thoughts I can subscribe to and work toward.

I also work with members of a local listserv that is mostly Republican and/or conservative. Many in this group homeschool their children and advocate for parental rights and responsibility. They also keep up on what is going on in public schools and work for positive change there.

Nationally, I subscribe to several email lists and several listservs from right to left and back again. In all these groups of people, there are those willing to work together to improve education for everyone.

A few years ago, I learned all about *zealots* at a community outreach seminar put on by my school district. Webster defines a *zealot* as "especially: a fanatical partisan." The advice given at the seminar I attended was: Steer clear! In order to do this, we must first establish in our minds that fine line between *enthusiastic passion* and outright *fanatical partisanship*. The differences can be very hard to see. However, a field study of educational activists does provide ample opportunity for practice.

An Internet friend here in Washington, who advocates the separation of school and state, enjoys drawing out the best or the worst in me and my philosophies. He has helped me more clearly define and express what I stand for. This gentleman—who chooses to remain anonymous—sent me into the fray of the SepSchooler listserv. The SepSchooler proclamation states: "I proclaim publicly that I favor ending government involvement in education." Plain and simple, they want government out of schools. On their listserv, I began by introducing myself as someone who believes in public schools. Honest or foolhardy, the damage was done. My friend later told me he didn't expect me to dive in headfirst. For a while, I thought they were going to eat me alive!

A couple of members of the list wondered why I thought it was my right to *steal* my neighbor's tax money to pay for my children's education. One person asked me repeatedly—and sometimes quite rudely—if I had even read the organization's belief statement. But there were others, many others, kinder, gentler, more understanding of the differences between one human being and another and willing to carry on dialogue with someone who didn't agree hook, line, and sinker with their vision.

Amidst the 400-plus posts surrounding my queries in less than a month, I learned quite a bit about how background and experience influence beliefs about education. Some SepSchoolers had horrible experiences in public schools. Some act on religious convictions. Some follow their political views, which tend to be Libertarian and suggest an absolute minimum of government involvement in the lives of citizens. I can respect, understand, and work with people who are doing what's best for their children and trying to help others who want what is best for theirs. The zealotry line is crossed when people insist on telling me they know better than I do what is best for *my* child. Sounds sort of like what goes on in some public/government schools, doesn't it?

Joining a listserv that holds a view that is somewhat in disagreement with your own can:

1. Help you to develop better listening abilities.
2. Teach you to be patient about asserting your views.
3. Force you to work on your debate skills.

Unless you enjoy trial by fire, I would suggest lurking—reading without writing or introducing yourself to the participants—for a while, so you don't become overwhelmed as I did with this first experience in what can be combative territory.

Books can also help in the area of people skills. One old standby, usually available in both new and used bookstores and every Goodwill in the nation, is Dale Carnegie's *How to Win Friends and Influence People*. I found another good people skills book, when I had spare time in the airport last summer, *Reading People, How to Understand People and Predict Their Behavior—Anytime, Anyplace*, by Jo-Ellan Dimitrius and Mark Mazzarella. Dr. Dimitrius works as a jury consultant and has "read" prospective jurors for cases as infamous as the O. J. Simpson criminal trial. Who better to teach me to tell if someone is an educational zealot?

Another book, *Taking Sides: Clashing Views on Controversial Educational Issues*, edited by James Wm. Noll, offers a debate format, grouping the essays of education scholars and theorists in pro and con pairs. It presents a good look at just how heated the discussion can get over a variety educational concepts.

John Dewey: Man or Beast?

I had to laugh out loud at a forum I was taking part in on our state's WASL test. The forum was cosponsored by a couple of teachers' unions and several groups of mostly progressive activists.

There was a table provided for those in attendance to display their literature. The WASL test is hated left and right in our state, for varying reasons, so there were many points of view and political directions represented in the crowded hall. One group had placed bookmarks on the table, which listed *The Schools We Need and Why We Don't Have Them,* by E. D. Hirsch, as a resource. E. D. Hirsch is the founder and chairman of the Core Knowledge Foundation <*www.coreknowledge.org/*> and believes in basic, common curriculum in public schools. This common curriculum often has a decidedly Christian and/or middle Anglo-Saxon America over- or undertone. Dr. Hirsch has also written numerous books in a series of *What Your First, Second, Third [etc.] Grader Should Know.* Undoubtedly, there are many good things in these books for some parents. Unfortunately, the authoritarian thinking of Dr. Hirsch is partly to blame for getting us into this standardized test-'em-to-death rut in the first place.

At any rate, the young master-of-ceremonies found it necessary to announce that the conference sponsors did not endorse these materials and did not know why they had been placed on the table. Just about then I was thinking a little chant of "Lean to the left; lean to the right; stand up; sit down; fight, fight, fight," would have been in order, followed by a few deep cleansing breaths.

Those promoting the rather prolific writings of Hirsh often complain that the *left* follows John Dewey—that early twentieth-century education philosopher, who worked on the idea of child-centered education and had a lot of suggestions about engaging children in learning, rather than boring them to death with just-the-facts-ma'am bookwork. Our more conservative brethren have a tendency to spew Dewey from their mouths—I never knew you!—just as Hirsch turns the stomachs of those who lean toward more progressive theory and practice.

Educational Bigotry in Three Words or Less

Unfortunately, people in powerful places—and sometimes in not so powerful places—often find it easier to label an educational philosophy than to fully understand and judge its usefulness. Once a derogatory title is attached, the battle lines are drawn and it becomes difficult for the rest of us to figure out what is going on. The following is by no means a complete list of the great divides in our current education culture.

- **Drill and Kill** My back-to-basics friends prefer to call this "drill for skill." To everything there is a season, and a time for every flashcard under heaven. It never hurt a child to memorize a multiplication table. It also never hurt a child to use the multiplication table in the inside of their notebook until they were in junior high. Memorization is a tool. So is a calculator. There is power in the memorization of a times table. Sometimes parents appreciate it when teachers spend time working with children to do just that.
- **Fuzzy Math** The "fuzzy" in "fuzzy math" is often brought about by crappy curriculum, thrown together to make a big buck. We all want our kids to understand math, but facts are facts. A favorite protest poster comment on the ridiculous grading policy for WASL math: "$2+3=4$, but I can explain." The idea that kids can get the wrong answer on a test and get more points, if they explain well, than they would if they got the right answer, but didn't explain how they got it, just sort of rubs many parents the wrong way. So does third-grade math homework that we can't understand.
- **Homeschooler** (said with a sneer, while rolling one's eyes, or worn on a J.C. Penney T-shirt) Many educational activists these days are homeschooling parents. The bureaucracy no longer allows for all involved parents to find what their kids need in their local public schools. The National Education Association frowns on homeschooling. But then, many homeschoolers frown on the NEA. It takes multiple programs and opportunity to teach all children. It's time for the rock throwing to stop!
- **Hole Language** (said while spitting on the ground—to your left) The problem with many educational theories is that they don't get thorough-enough practice. Lack of resources and poor communication cause failure. Programs become watered down by little or no professional development. It's important to look at the potential for any program and see that it is put to its best use. Put the "whole" back in whole language. I have

questioned the whole language experts. True whole language involves the most basic of all instructional materials—real books! It also includes letter sounds, grammar, and word and language use and meaning.

■ **Fonix** (also said while spitting on the ground—to your right) The government reading reform of choice, direct-instruction phonics, will not serve all the children all the time. However, some of us parent, teacher, and student types actually do perform best in a neatly structured, row-and-column world.

■ **Grade Inflation** Just imagine, big puffy As and Bs handed out to children who only deserve a flat-lining C or D. Egad! Get those grades and those touchy-feely, child-nurturing teachers under control! When the local banker runs the state academic achievement commission, the stories of kids with high school diplomas not being able to pass the teller test abound. The human enterprise of education requires that human teachers use their best judgment and award grades based on the performance and abilities of the whole child. If we remove the ability of teachers to set and temper grades, we remove the compassion from thirteen years of mandatory education.

10 Work to Improve Social Realities

R-E-S-P-E-C-T

One day while playing on our swing set with my twins, the three of us were carrying on a nice conversation. Carmen and Samuel were about three years old, and it was one of those Sunday mornings when I had sent the rest of the family off to church and stayed home to enjoy my toddlers rather than attempting to corral and keep them quiet in a church pew. I was showing them how I could swing very high, and they seemed to think this was a little silly. I said, "Big people can swing, too."

"You're not a people; you're a mommy!" was Samuel's insightful retort.

This statement came back to me the other day, as I was thinking about the idea of respect in our schools. Too often, today's leaders in education take on the attitude of my three-year-old son, saying in a variety of ways, "You're not a people; you're a parent," or "you're a teacher," or "you're a student." The lack of respect for those in the position to best understand children and their needs is astounding.

Our society at large decided, years ago, that parenting could be done in off-hours and spare time. *Stay-at-home-mom* became a lackluster, and, in many cases, economically challenged concept. We are feeling the affects. Now, coming to a 21st century near you, witness the demolition of the teaching profession. Raise your hand if you've heard the term *teacher-proof curriculum*.

Behold the attitude exuded by the Business Roundtable and those in the education government who kowtow to their whims:

> You teachers are too subjective, too human. You can't be trusted to know what's right for children. We'll bring in eighteen-year-old volunteers to direct you teachers in before- and after-school tutoring of the children you have in your classes six hours a day. Parents aren't doing what's right, either, so we'll do you all the favor of creating universal pre-school and scripted K-12. We have new research on brain development and scientifically proven curriculum that we think should be applied.

The issue of respect never seems to be addressed—by anyone. The education government displays little respect for the student, parent, teacher, or taxpayer. There are enough parents out here who believe in public schools and public school teachers that the system should work for most kids and families—and in most places it does, despite the rantings of the hierarchy and the scare tactics of educational risk reports.

So, what's happening when and where public education isn't working? In many areas, it is a simple lack of resources that cause the failure. There is no mystery of the ills of public schools and student achievement that will be revealed by nationally mandated tests in grades three through eight. What these tests reveal is that poor children in poor schools do poorly. We have seen the light! What they further reveal is that improving communication, parent and teacher support, and resources—sometimes a resource boost as simple and economical as feeding children a $1 breakfast before testing—improves test scores. Hallelujah!

It has become common for test-pushers to label test-resisters *unfeeling elitists*. This is quite ironic, considering the effects of the tests in further labeling poor children and schools. To throw a little mud back at the test-scores-as-revelation crowd, in the words of Bill Cosby, "They must be HIGH!" Or perhaps they are just blind and ignorant. Perhaps they don't read reports on school facilities and human resource needs of low-income communities. Perhaps they feel that *those kids* would just ruin good facilities and wear out qualified teachers anyway. Perhaps they feel that *those kids* need more discipline and structure, but they can do without books, clean water supplies, and roofs that don't leak. Perhaps they see no need

Figure 10–1 Stop Look Listen

to direct educational resources to kids and communities, rather than to the four major testing and curriculum companies, for test development, test administration, curriculum alignment, and data disaggregation.

At a recent accountability meeting, Washington State's federal education liaison—every state has one—was crooning a data tune about the needs for bigger and better computer systems to file and sort and rank and order children and their abilities. I sat there wondering: Who burned her copy of *1984?*

"But, what about those really rotten parents and those really rotten teachers?" you say.

"Name names and count the percentages," I say. When polls are taken, parents are generally happy with the schools their children attend. Most worry about schools in other communities, however. My prescription for school evaluation and improvement on a local level is simple, and it is stated on the back of my activist card.

Parents who feel that their concerns are heard and that they have choices for their children within the system are more apt to support and be involved in schools. Teachers who have the needed resources and feel their work is appreciated automatically do a better job for kids. *Educational empathy,* understanding the needs of all those involved in education, is the most powerful of all school improvement tools.

Finding ways to empower teachers and parents for the good of kids is our society's greatest challenge in the next few years. Holding our breath and making a wish for light at the end of the tunnel is not an option. The only viable alternative to data collection is human engagement. We improve schools by helping one person at a time. We help one person at a time by

- Appreciating effort
- Voicing encouragement
- Offering assistance
- Speaking up when we see an injustice

Top-down Accountability

My friend and fellow Mother Against WASL, Jean Ward, and I had dinner one evening with our state superintendent, Terry Bergeson. A telling moment came when I looked Dr. Bergeson in the eyes and said, "It's all about communication."

"You're right, Juanita," she said.

Okay, she does know the answer to the mess we're in!

What's the problem, then? Where does communication break down? Is the system too big? Are parents not paying attention? Are teachers overburdened? Is the administration of the *system* more important to the state than the success of the *student*? How is the money spent? Does communication mean slick Partnership for Learning pamphlets meant to schmooze us into thinking big improvements are being made, all the while our rights over our children's education are being stripped away?

Funny thing about time and money: the farther the spending is from the classroom, the more money there seems to be and the more time it seems to buy in the form of consultants, assistants, specialists, and experts.

I've worked on many funding committees at the building and district level. My district is in the process of building a new high school and junior high. Between county codes, state funding formulas, federal programming guidelines, and community planning, wasteful spending on the part of district officials is not an option. In fact, any wiggle-room we included in the carefully planned budget has been eaten up by the cost of purchasing water rights we thought we had, relocating a wetland, and improving a road that was supposed to have been improved by the state—they ran out of money!

The directors of our district projects spend the hard-earned and long-fought-for bond money as if it was their own, very carefully taking bids and saving dollars whenever they can, in case unexpected costs arise. They report to the local citizen's committee and school board, as well as county and state officials. There is an abundance of accountability at the district level. In fact, the entire, tedious process serves to slow down the construction of the schools which we already needed years ago in our fast-growing district.

Recently, it was discovered that the roofs of four elementary schools must be rebuilt, because weather conditions and the design of the roofs has created a problem with mold. A nearby district is closing an elementary that was making students and staff sick for this very reason. In order to keep from having to close our schools in the near future, these roofs must be rebuilt now, using funds meant for other projects. A problem with the water supply in my children's school and the elementary and high school that share the same system has sent notes home to parents recently, telling of contaminants and the need for bottled water, which the district will provide. It is a constant juggling of priorities—roofs to keep out mold or improvements to the water supply system? Of course, these two items are not optional, so the new rugs to replace those that are worn out and tripping kids, the new lock systems to improve school security, and the storage units for emergency supplies, in case of earthquake or other very possible catastrophes, will be put off indefinitely.

Regardless of how frustrated I may feel when a note from school tells me my children can't drink the water for a few days or when projects must be rearranged by district officials to fix the most pressing problems first, these are quite middle-class inconveniences compared to the conditions of schools in more needy areas.

A recent lawsuit filed against the state of California, on behalf of students attending eighteen different schools around the state, listed the facilities, supplies, and staff requirements the state did not provide to fulfill its constitutional guarantee of basic education. An ACLU press release listed "Degraded, Unhealthful Facilities and Conditions."

- Broken or nonexistent air conditioning or heating systems
- Toilets that don't flush
- Toilets that are locked
- Broken windows, walls, and ceilings
- Vermin infestations
- Leaky roofs and mold

The press release quotes teacher Shannon Carey, "This January 14, the roof in my classroom leaked over half of my room, ruining a great many diligently done projects. The roof had been leaking for years—fourteen years, in fact—and yet not one repair was undertaken to prevent its eventual collapse."

"Chronically unfilled teacher vacancies" are listed in the column labeled: "Inadequate Instruction," which raises the question: Just how devoted does a teacher like Shannon Carey have to be to guide students to work *diligently* on projects, in conditions so bad that the roof caves in? The presidential answer to all this: *Let them eat tests!* See ACLU-NC Press Release May 17, 2000, <*www.aclunc.org/ pressrel/000517-schools.html*>.

In contrast to district funding, state-level frivolities seem to abound: $100,000 here for governor-signed certificates of accomplishment to students for test scores, $200,000 there for a teacher test-scoring field trip to Arizona. Here a million, there a million, everywhere another million, which adds up to a lot of money that could be spent on the basic needs of schools. Somehow, if we can't afford a roof over our heads and a teacher in every classroom, the whole strategically planned show becomes nothing but a tragedy of errors.

I am currently studying a $62-million, five-year contract with the state's testing company of choice and receipts from an airfare budget that seems to keep the state superintendent state-hopping rather than tending to the real needs of schools in Washington State. I am far from alone in my thoughts that the testing bureaucracy is sapping needed funds from local schools. Teachers' unions in both California and Washington recently called for a halt or scale back in state testing programs as state legislators talk of cutting school funding in response to economic woes.

Following the money is one of the easiest, though time-consuming, ways to discover the priorities of education leaders.

- Start with your state education website and locate funding/ budget documents there. These should include district budgets and spending as well as state level allocations. There are many places to find your state's education department website, but one easy resource is the National Council for Accreditation of Teacher Education site, which maintains links for every state at <www.ncate.org/resources/statelinks.htm>.
- Look into public disclosure documents and see who supports the campaigns of your elected education officials. The California Voter Foundation has assembled a list of state disclosure websites and campaign finance data at <www.digitalsunlight .org/disclosurelinkschart.html>.
- Utilize freedom of information laws to request copies of contracts, invoices, and any other items that would be relevant to your particular area of concern. A good website to find information about state and federal freedom of information procedures, including information request form letters, is maintained by the National Freedom of Information Coalition at <www.nfoic.org>.

Having the Freedom of Information laws on your side doesn't mean there won't be roadblocks. The day I traveled to the Office of the Superintendent of Public Instruction to help my friend Nancy Vernon copy the files she had requested, she and I were greeted by a strange situation. Those in charge at the superintendent's office were not going to allow me to go with Nancy to the room where they had assembled the documents for her. When I arrived in the lobby, Nancy phoned the attorney general's office while I wrote out a note of my own to gain access to the documents she had requested under the public access laws.

Within a few minutes, the attorney general's office had phoned those in the area we would be working and I was given permission to enter. Knowing your rights and your state law and being assertive can make a big difference when those in charge don't seem to understand them.

Once in the conference room, where Nancy and I were allowed to work, we began copying file upon file of expenditure receipts and contracts with curriculum and testing companies, professional development providers, and travel agents. The documentation is all there and it is available to the public, as required by law. Holding our public servants accountable for their spending habits will take time, but it can be done. As Nancy digs through files and passes on to me what she thinks I can use, we will be able to show the public just how much money is spent outside the classroom. True, worthwhile accountability begins with those who control funding.

Just after I met Nancy, she filed an ethics complaint with the state auditor, naming our state superintendent and an assistant superintendent who was working for a company, Sopris West, which was selling teacher training services to the state at the same time she was working for the state. Nancy's investigation has now resulted in a $10,000 ethics penalty, plus $5,000 to cover the costs of the state investigation—the largest ever in Washington State—against the assistant superintendent. Sopris West will also pay $20,000 to the state education department as a result of Nancy's complaint. When reporters asked Nancy how much time and money she had spent on her investigation, she couldn't tell them. We have just begun to fight!

Interesting things come to light when we *little people* get a look at what's going on in the state capitol or the state education building. Something seems to happen to people once they are running the show and are part of big government. It's time to turn the table and start shouting, "Accountability now!" back at our state officials.

Local Control Is Where It's At!

The farther educational decisions get away from the teacher, the parent, and the child, the more apt they are to be wrong. I keep repeating this statement in every interview and forum, hoping its meaning will take hold and the word will spread. It is a well-known fact that the farther data is taken from the original collection point, the more forgetful everyone becomes about the circumstances under which it was collected. Considering this, I suppose it makes sense that our Washington test is graded in Arizona, the original answer sheets shredded, and the scores returned four months later, when children have moved on to different teachers or, in many cases, different school districts. This makes it easier for state officials to claim the scores are valid, regardless of district, school, and child circumstances. They call this, "No excuses."

Our schools are not factories that dispense a standard product where quality control, clad in plastic gloves, pulls rejects from the conveyor belt and offers them for sale in outlet stores. When children no longer need nurturing from teachers, grades can become completely objective. Until then, value will vary, and students will learn to work with a variety of human expectations in a course of thirteen years spent with dozens of teachers. I found some hope recently at a meeting of our State House Education Committee, when one of the representatives actually pointed out that for all its human frailty and fallibility, grade point average is still a better tool than an SAT score in predicting college success. Comparison studies by the College Board confirm this fact.

Many states are instituting accountability plans that will allow for state takeover of elected school boards and locally hired administrators and teachers. The federal government has also enacted legislation that includes these takeover consequences. Am I missing something, or am I right in observing that this is a usurping of our democratic system of government? This isn't just something that's happening in those backward states with those rotten schools. (Hey, you, this week's poster states for educational neglect—you know who you are and shame on you.) We're all in this together!

The governor of Vermont figured out that, according to scores on state-designed tests, the federal government would label 30 percent of his state's schools failing, even though Vermont students score above average on national standardized tests such as the National Assessment of Educational Progress. Where does that leave states that are below the national average?

Certainly, we want schools to prepare children for adult life, including college and/or work. Local business people and community organizations should have some input to what goes on in schools. It is understandable that business leaders would be interested in education, even to the point where they would want to help with innovative programs or offer apprenticeships. We should all get more than a little nervous, however, when CEOs of companies like IBM and State Farm begin dictating to governors and other state and national officials that they had better get education whipped into shape, and dictating just what shape that will be. Standards-Based Education is an educational philosophy or theory—and it's rapidly becoming a universally omnipotent education philosophy or theory. A look at any state education website will demonstrate this fact loud and clear. Standards! We must have standards!

The Business Roundtable and Achieve, Inc., websites are interesting places to visit—to study the overlapping names, for one thing—but I wouldn't want to live there or have them directing my children's future, though they seem to be doing that already.

A quote from the opening page of Achieve, Inc., <*www.achieve.org*>: "Achieve, Inc., is an independent, bipartisan, nonprofit organization that helps states raise academic standards, measure performance against those standards, establish clear accountability for results and strengthen public confidence in our education system." Perhaps as recession hits and we watch the mighty fall in the world of business, our schools can help restore confidence in The Business Roundtable. See <*www.brt.org*> if you'd like to help.

Lest anyone get the idea that Achieve, Inc., is ruled by any one political party, here is its statement on political makeup: "Achieve's board of directors is composed of six governors (three Democrats and three Republicans) and six CEOs." When big money and big business are involved, party lines seem to smear like so much chalk dust.

Local control has flown out the classroom window—or door. Read the words of Louis Gerstner, Jr., CEO of IBM, cochair of Achieve, Inc., and member of the Business Roundtable, spoken at this year's Education Summit—a meeting involving business CEOs and their hand-picked education leaders and governors—in Palisades, N.Y.: "Standards and assessments were the right start, but they're not all we need. So in 1999, we agreed to a new set of actions. As we said at the time, 'to drive standards from the Achieve website through the schoolhouse door.' Again, two overriding commitments: Agreement on the urgent need for a vastly improved teaching profession; and curricula that could actually move our kids to the achievement level that is commonplace in the rest of the developed world."

It is interesting to note the ease with which the achievement of "the rest of the developing world" is touted. If one does an in-depth

Figure 10–2 Thanks anyway, guys.

study of international math and science competition, most of our United States are right up there scoring with the best in the world as is the United States as a whole. Yet, only Canada and the United States offer free public education to every child. Perhaps by "improve the teaching profession," Mr. Gerstner means to create teachers who know how to rebuild roofs or hold up ceiling tiles with one hand while they hold the book and teach from scripted lessons with the other.

From the Business Roundtable "Reform 2001" page: "For the past 12 years, The Business Roundtable has been involved in an unprecedented effort to improve education in the states. This year, the BRT is helping to shape education policy at the national level as well." The page ends with the proud banner: "Education is Everybody's Business." There you have it.

I'm positive I can do a better job of educating my children with the help of my local schools, without the direction of CEOs Philip Condit, Boeing; Craig Barrett, Intel; Edward Rust, Jr., State Farm;

Arthur Ryan, Prudential; Keith Bailey, Williams; and Lou Gerstner, Jr., IBM. Thanks anyway, guys.

Maybe I would be more impressed with the good hearts of these business leaders if they worried a little more about the thousands of parents being laid off in the downsizing of companies on American soil and a little less about what reading program is used in my child's American classroom.

It's time for parents, teachers, and local community members everywhere to gang up and take back *our* schools.

Parents Are Responsible for the Education of Their Children

In order for children to get the most out of their education, parents must be involved. Institutions cannot raise children, and it is questionable whether they can educate them. Parents must be the final quality control and the overseers of their child's learning.

Parents who are concerned about education and adequately involved in the lives of their children often find alternatives to the neighborhood school, for one reason or another. In our technologically adept society, many families are choosing computer-based alternatives within the public school system. In Washington State alone, there are 20,000 homeschooled children. Parents are not required to file an "Intent to Homeschool" with their local district until a child is eight years old, so this number is probably quite understated.

An agenda of vouchers and school choice exists at the national level and in many states. Whether lessening community support and the push toward educational competition present problems for our schools depends on how individual schools and districts choose to approach the subject of parental and community involvement. A handful of parents working on PTA fundraisers and room-mothering at Valentine's parties doesn't hack it anymore—and probably never did.

We are told that our children need new and better skills than we ever needed, but there is nothing new under the sun. Adaptation to technology and the communication age, if that's what *they* are talking about, is a process of natural curiosity. Don't take my word for it. Put a five-year-old in a room with a computer and see what happens.

Those pushing the panic buttons of technological literacy, upper-level thinking skills, global economy, and the need to collaborate in the workplace forget that the twentieth century brought us such innovations and changes in lifestyle as electricity, cars, airplanes, universal indoor plumbing, and two-income households.

Change is a human condition, but children need the same things today as children have always needed. Caring adults to nurture and encourage them is the first requirement. A variety of experiences and teaching strategies round out the child-care package nicely.

Let's make a bold assumption: if parents are asked what we want for our child, we will never say we want them to read on a second-grade level in seventh grade. We will never say that we want them to drop out at fourteen and sell drugs. We will never say we want them to assault a teacher and end up in that alternative school for the "bad kids."

I have a dream that someday all parents will be greeted at the school door and asked, as the priest or minister does when a child is baptized, "What do you ask for this child?" The answer: A school that is clean and safe, teachers who care about my kid and have time to teach, homework that doesn't take three hours a night to complete, good communication, respect, and NO JARGON! Seems to me these are mostly the same things teachers want for children.

I've guesstimated that my four children have, so far, experienced the care and teaching of nearly 100 teachers in public schools. I can count on less than one hand the teachers who did not do a good job of teaching. My mother used to say that one can learn something from every teacher—even if it's how *not* to teach. My children haven't learned how not to teach from very many of their teachers.

I suppose some would say our family has been extremely lucky, but I prefer to believe that the majority of teachers in the majority of the schools in our country are doing a good job working with young people.

Schools for the 21st century need:

1. Family involvement
2. Community support
3. Adequate human resources and funding
4. Competent administration

It's as simple and as complicated, as progressive and as traditional as that.

Appendix 1:
The Activist's Cookbook

Kiss-up Cookies (absolutely mood-altering)

Heat oven to 375°. Place in large mixer bowl and mix on medium
speed until well blended:

The big batch

1 lb real margarine (not that
watery "spread" stuff)

1½ cups granulated sugar

1½ cups brown sugar (packed)

3 large eggs

2 teaspoons vanilla

1½ teaspoons baking soda

1½ teaspoons salt

The smaller batch

1⅓ cups margarine

1 cup granulated sugar

1 cup brown sugar (packed)

2 large eggs

1½ teaspoon vanilla

1 teaspoon baking soda

1 teaspoon salt

On low speed, add 1 cup at a time and mix in until well blended:

4½ cups all-purpose flour   3 cups all-purpose flour

Still on low speed, mix in:

3 cups old-fashioned oats   2 cups old-fashioned oats

Stir in your choice(s) of the following:

12–18 ounces chocolate chips   12 ounces chocolate chips

12 ounces M&Ms   6–10 ounces M&Ms

The big batch	The smaller batch
10–12 ounces white chocolate chips	10–12 ounces white chocolate chips
1½ cups dried cranberries	1 cup dried cranberries
1½ cups macadamia nuts	1 cup macadamia nuts
1½ cups walnuts	1 cup walnuts

Drop dough by spoonfuls (you pick the size) on an ungreased baking sheet. Bake (375°) for 7–12 minutes, depending on your oven and the size of your spoonfuls.

For large cookies, dough should be flattened slightly before baking to prevent uneven baking. Remove to cooling rack.

Slap in the Face Frosting (a mind of its own)

In small mixing bowl, stir on medium speed until blended:

1 lb powdered sugar

1 stick margarine (½ cup)

¼ cup milk

When ingredients are evenly moistened, beat on high speed until smooth. Add food coloring as desired. This recipe makes enough to frost one boxed cake mix or several dozen cookies. Practice writing dissident messages. Find some deserving child or spouse to eat your mistakes.

Sugar Cookies for the Board (the perfect canvas for your frosting art)

The big batch! Dough may be frozen for later use. Baked cookies may be frozen for later frosting and eating. Mix and beat well with electric mixer:

2¼ cups margarine

3 cups sugar

6 eggs

1 tablespoon vanilla

1 tablespoon baking powder

1 tablespoon salt

Slowly add and blend in:

7½ cups flour

Chill dough at least 2 hours. Roll dough ⅛–¼ inch thick on well-floured surface. Cut with desired cookie cutters. Carefully place cookies approximately one inch apart on ungreased cookie sheet. Bake 5–7 minutes in 400° oven. Remove from cookie sheet and cool. Frost appropriately.

Makes about 12 dozen cookies.

Bite Me Banana Bread (throw them some rotten fruit)

Mix and set aside:

2⅓ cups flour

1 cup coarsely chopped nuts (your choice, I use walnuts or pecans)

1 cup dried cranberries

1 teaspoon baking powder

1 teaspoon baking soda

¼ teaspoon salt

In another large bowl, mix with electric mixer until well blended:

 2½ cups sugar

 1 cup mashed ripe banana

 2 teaspoons vanilla

 2 eggs

Add and mix well:

 1 cup melted margarine (cooled)

 1 cup buttermilk

By hand, stir in flour mixture until evenly moistened. Bake at 350°, in a greased and floured pan (or pans) of your choice.

 Baking time will vary with size of pans—small pans 30 minutes; large pans, up to 1 hour. Cool bread 15 minutes in pan before removing. Bread freezes well for later use. If desired, dust top of bread with powdered sugar or glaze with a powdered sugar/water glaze. Makes 1 large bundt cake or 2 rectangular loaves.

I D'eclairs! (impress the heck out of them)

Bring to a boil in a large saucepan:

 1 cup margarine

 2 cups water

Over low heat, stir in until smooth (a wire whisk works well):

 2 cups flour

Remove pan from heat. Whisk in until smooth:

 4 eggs

Place dough in a baker's piping bag (these are available in the cake decorating sections of most variety stores or at kitchen specialty shops). Opening in bag should be approximately 1 inch in diameter. Pipe dough in 3-inch lines on ungreased baking sheet. Bake at 400° for approximately 30 minutes, or until puffy and lightly browned. Remove pastries to cooling rack. When cool, slice off tops and fill vanilla pudding, below. Replace tops of pastries and glaze with chocolate glaze, below. Place éclairs in pastry or cupcake papers to serve.

Vanilla Pudding:

Prepare 1 small package instant vanilla pudding according to instructions on box, substituting for required milk:

1½ cups milk

½ cup sour cream or imitation sour cream

Chocolate Glaze

Stir together:

3 tablespoons dry cocoa

1 tablespoon melted margarine

1 cup powdered sugar

Hot water for desired consistency (1–2 tablespoons)

Knead-Out-Your-Frustration Cinnamon Rolls

Place in a large bowl and stir together:

10 cups all purpose flour

2 pkg. Rapid-Rise yeast

6 tablespoons sugar

1½ tablespoon salt

Heat to 130°: (the only time I use my microwave temperature probe)

> 3 cups water
>
> 1 cup milk
>
> ⅓ cup vegetable oil

Pour liquid into bowl of dry ingredients. Stir with a spoon until ingredients are evenly moistened. Pour onto floured board. Knead it like you mean it for 10 minutes, or until dough is smooth and soft.

Add flour as needed so that dough is not sticky. (This may take as much as 2–3 cups of additional flour.) Place dough in large, well-greased (margarine, butter, or shortening) bowl, turning once to coat with greasing substance. Cover with light towel and place in a warm oven (100–120°) for approximately 1 hour, or until doubled. Punch the dough down, and let it sit covered for 10 minutes.

While dough sits, melt:

> ½ cup butter or margarine

Dump dough on a lightly floured surface and separate into two equal pieces.

Roll or pat half of dough into a rectangle, so that dough is about ¾ inch thick.

Drizzle or brush dough with half the melted margarine. Sprinkle dough with:

> ½ cup granulated or brown sugar
>
> A generous amount of cinnamon
>
> Lots of raisins or other dried or candied fruit, if desired

Roll dough like a jelly roll, starting at the long edge.
Take a 1½-foot piece of sewing thread and slide it under the roll of dough. Cut 1-inch rolls by pulling the ends of the thread up and together. Place rolls slightly apart in a well-greased baking pan. Cover with light towel. Repeat with second half of dough. Place pans in a

warm (100–120°) oven, until rolls are almost doubled. Remove from oven and remove towels. Heat oven to 350°. Bake rolls 10–15 minutes, or until golden brown. Remove to cooling rack or serve hot.

Frost if desired, with canned frosting or stir together:

2 cups powdered sugar

1 tablespoon softened margarine

Enough milk to thin to desired consistency

I said, "Wassail" not "WASL," punch

The day (or longer) before: Mix one package unsweetened red Kool-Aid with one quart of water. Do not add sugar. Freeze in a ring mold (a bundt-cake pan or gelatin mold will work).
Time to party: Place ice-ring in punchbowl. Pour in equal amounts of orange juice and any lemon-lime carbonated soft-drink. Ring will usually last through at least two liters of each. If you will need more than one punch ring and you have only one mold, freeze them ahead of time and place frozen rings in a zip-lock bag in freezer.

Why Do They Act Like Such Noodles? Salad (for teachers' lounge potlucks)

12 oz. package multicolored pasta, cooked, drained, and cooled

6 oz. can black olives, drained and cut in half lengthwise

1 cup celery sliced diagonally

1 sweet red or green pepper, sliced thinly

red onion, sliced thinly (optional, amount may vary)

10 oz. frozen petite peas, thawed

1 cucumber cut in half lengthwise and thinly sliced, peel on or off

1 cup julienned ham (optional)

1 large bottle or prepared packet Italian dressing (no-fat variety may be used)

Toss all ingredients gently in a large bowl. For attractive serving, line serving bowl with red leaf lettuce.

Appendix 2: Resource Gallery

Website Favorites

Help and information

Amazon sells books. *<www.amazon.com>*

The Association for Supervision and Curriculum Development is a good source for up-to-date articles. *<www.ascd.org>*

Barnes and Noble also sells books. *<www.bn.com>*

Café Press prints and sells your design on T-shirts, mugs, mouse pads, etc. at no charge to you. *<www.cafepress.com>*

The California Voter Foundation has assembled a list of state disclosure websites and campaign finance information. *<www.digital sunlight.org/disclosurelinkschart.html>*

Education Week on the web offers an excellent list of education organizations, grouped by category—administrators, service and volunteer, philanthropy and grants. *<www.edweek.org/context/ orgs/orgs.htm>*

Google is the mother of all search engines. *<www.google.com>*

Internet Nonprofit Center offers everything you ever wanted to know about nonprofits but were too busy to call and ask. *<www.nonprofits.org>*

National Center for Education Statistics features data on public schools in a searchable format. Go there to find downloads or order a single copy—disc or book form—of any available report, for free, including *The Condition of Education Yearbook*. *<www.nces.ed.gov>*

National Council for Accreditation of Teacher Education maintains links for every state education department. *<www.ncate.org/ resources/statelinks.htm>*

National Freedom of Information Coalition offers state and national public information laws. <www.nfoic.org>

Net Action has a training guide for the Virtual Activist; advice and links to more advice on the web-based approach to activism. <www.netaction.org/training/>

Newslink will help you find just about any news source in the world. <www.newslink.org>

Phi Delta Kappa and *Kappan* magazine are good sources for a variety of thoughts on timely education subjects. <www.pdkintl.org>

U.S. Department of Education has a bounty of links to legislation, state and local schools, educational resources, etc. <www.ed.gov/index.jsp>

A few friends and fellow activists—representing a rainbow of political spectrum and educational specialties you can judge for yourself

Alliance for Childhood <www.allianceforchildhood.org>

California Coalition for Authentic Reform in Education <www.calcare.org>

Citizens United for Responsible Education <www.curewashington.org>

FairTest <www.fairtest.org>

Alfie Kohn <www.alfiekohn.org>

Maple River Education Coalition PAC <mredcopac.org>

Mass Refusal <www.massrefusal.org>

National Coalition of Education Activists <www.nceaonline.org>

No More Tests <www.nomoretests.com>

Susan Ohanian <www.susanohanian.org>

Parent Directed Education <www.parentdirectededucation.org>

Pencils Down <www.pencilsdown.org>

Rethinking Schools <www.rethinkingschools.org/index.html>

The Rouge Forum <www.pipeline.com/~rgibson/rouge_forum>

Teachers Getting Active <www.teachersmatter.com>

Bookshelf

Berliner, David C., James Bell, and Bruce J. Biddle. 1996. *The Manufactured Crisis: Myths, Fraud and Attack on America's Public Schools.* Cambridge, MA: Perseus Books.

Bracey, Gerald W. 2001. *The War Against America's Public Schools: Privatizing Schools, Commercializing Education.* Boston: Allyn and Bacon.

Carnegie, Dale. 1976. *How to Develop Self-Confidence and Influence People by Public Speaking.* New York: Simon and Schuster.

———. 1982. *How to Win Friends and Influence People* (revised edition). New York: Simon and Schuster.

Dimitrius, Jo-Ellan, and Mark Mazzarella. 1999. *Reading People: How to Understand People and Predict Their Behavior—Anytime, Anyplace.* New York: Ballantine Books.

Elkind, David. 1988. *Miseducation: Preschoolers at Risk.* New York: Alfred A. Knopf.

Goodlad, John I. 1984. *A Place Called School.* New York: McGraw-Hill.

Hoy, Wayne, and Cecil Miskel. 2000. *Educational Administration: Theory, Research, and Practice.* Columbus, OH: McGraw-Hill Higher Education.

Kohn, Alfie. 2000. *The Case Against Standardized Testing: Raising the Scores, Ruining the Schools.* Portsmouth, NH: Heinemann.

Kozol, Jonathan. 1992. *Savage Inequalities.* New York: HarperCollins.

Kralovec, Etta, and John Buell. 2000. *The End of Homework: How Homework Disrupts Families, Overburdens Children, and Limits Learning.* Boston: Beacon Press.

Krashen, Stephen D. 1999. *Condemned Without a Trial: Bogus Arguments Against Bilingual Education.* Portsmouth, NH: Heinemann.

———. 1999. *Three Arguments Against Whole Language and Why They Are Wrong.* Portsmouth, NH: Heinemann.

Lane, Mary B. 2001. *Democratic Schools for Our Democracy.* Lincoln, NE: iUniverse, Inc.

Meier, Deborah. 1995. *The Power of Their Ideas.* Boston: Beacon Press.

Noll, James W., ed. 2000. *Taking Sides: Clashing Views on Controversial Educational Issues.* McGraw-Hill Higher Education.

———. 1996. *The End of Education: Redefining the Value of Schools.* New York: Alfred A. Knopf.

Ohanian, Susan. 2001. *Caught in the Middle: Nonstandard Kids and a Killing Curriculum.* Portsmouth, NH: Heinemann.

———. 1999. *One Size Fits Few: The Folly of Educational Standards.* Portsmouth, NH: Heinemann.

———. 2002. *What Happened to Recess and Why Are Our Children Struggling in Kindergarten?* New York: McGraw-Hill.

Orlich, Donald C., Robert J. Harder, Richard C. Callahan, and Harry W. Gibson. 2001. *Teaching Strategies: A Guide to Better Instruction.* Boston: Houghton Mifflin Company.

Pipkin, Gloria, and Releah Cossett Lent. 2002. *At the Schoolhouse Gate: Lessons in Intellectual Freedom.* Portsmouth, NH: Heinemann.

Postman, Neil. 1994. *The Disappearance of Childhood.* New York: Random House.

Sacks, Peter. 1999. *Standardized Minds: The High Price of America's Testing Culture and What We Can Do to Change It.* Cambridge, MA: Perseus Books.

▄Appendix 3:
Sample Communication Tools

Sample Press Release

FOR IMMEDIATE RELEASE   Contact: Gloria Pipkin
July 2, 2001   850-265-6438
                                       gpipkin@I-1.net

"Spay the FCAT," Says Grassroots Group;
Tampa Rally to Kick Off Campaign

Concerned about the negative effects of test-based school reform, a group of parents and teachers from around the state have organized a grassroots group that seeks to reduce or eliminate the emphasis currently placed on the Florida Comprehensive Assessment Test. The Florida Coalition for Assessment Reform, Inc., (FCAR) kicks off its anti-FCAT campaign in Tampa on July 13 with a 10 AM rally at Courthouse Square Park.

"FCAT cannibalizes the curriculum, diverts scarce resources, discriminates against those who don't test well, and turns schools into giant test prep centers," said Gloria Pipkin of Lynn Haven, FCAR coordinator. "And it's a secret test. High-stakes decisions about graduation and promotion are being based on a test that parents aren't allowed to see," Pipkin said.

Dr. Joan Kaywell, professor of English education at the University of South Florida, called the FCAT "the worst educational quick-fix that the government has ever tried to implement." Kaywell, a Florida native, announced recently that she is leaving the state and moving to New Hampshire to protect her son from a test-driven curriculum.

Hillsborough Teacher of the Year Christie Gold reeled off a catalog of ill effects of FCAT. "Teachers at my school will once again sacrifice solid curriculum to chase the testing windmill. They will eliminate book talks, games of Literary Jeopardy, spelling bees, and geometric art projects in order to drill for a test that reveals nothing about student progress, achievement, or ability."

ReLeah Lent, a teacher in Bay County, provided more evidence of how FCAT deprives students of rich educational experiences. Lent wrote a grant to take her students to a touring production of *The Miracle Worker,* but the producer cancelled the show and said the company probably wouldn't come back to Florida, because teachers were too busy preparing for the FCAT to make time for field trips. Lent said, "It made me wonder what score Helen Keller would have made on the test."

Florida Council Teachers of English (FCTE) Beginning English Teacher of the Year Award Recipient (2000–2001) Lynne Grigelevich of Pasco County termed the FCAT "poisonous" in its effects on her students' sense of wonder and creativity.

Speaking out against the FCAT can be dangerous to a teacher's career, as Shannon Dosh, a graduate student at USF, learned during her first year of teaching. Dosh's principal refused her request to allow her students to write letters to the Governor about the FCAT. When Dosh's students challenged FCAT reading workbook questions, she was told to "teach to the test." Dosh was not rehired, and she believes she was terminated because she stood up for her students' rights to learn freely, outside the FCAT box.

Since its inception a few months ago FCAR has been primarily an Internet-based advocacy and support group, but this summer the organization will launch a series of rallies around the state, beginning in Tampa. The goal of these events is to call attention to the harms of FCAT, give voice to those whose concerns have gone unheard, and organize the resistance into a force for constructive change.

Sample Event Announcement

Teachers, Parents, Students, Grandparents, Aunts, Uncles Join in the Second Annual

Mothers and Others Walk Against WASL!

When:	1:00 PM Saturday, April 20, 2002
Where:	Meet at Bottom of the Capitol Steps to walk to the Old Capitol Building (OSPI) Olympia
Why:	To Declare Freedom from State-Mandated, High-Stakes Testing
Information:	Juanita Doyon Jedoyon@aol.com 253/846-0823

During spring testing season, educational justice groups across America will be holding events to call for a stop to high-stakes testing. Please join us in supporting this nationwide effort.

Figure A–3 Walk Against WASL Flyer

Sample Letter to the Editor

Juanita Doyon
20421 4ᵗʰ Ave E
Spanaway, WA 98387
253/846–0823
April 20, 2002

Hometown Newspaper
Subject: WASL Reasoning
265 words

To the Editor:

As a leader in the growing revolt against the Washington Assessment of Student Learning (WASL), I have counseled parents and students throughout the state concerning their right to opt out of the test. Many schools are very reasonable and simply accept a parent-signed note and provide alternative activities during testing times. Unfortunately, a few districts have found it appropriate to use coercion, scare tactics, and outright lies to get students to take the test and parents to change their minds about opting them out.

At the request of frustrated parents, I have developed a short position statement. Supporting evidence can be found in books and articles on testing, and in the public records concerning WASL itself. However, the following should suffice to quiet even the most obstinate school official:

The WASL is a wasteful, invalid, unproven, abusive experiment. My child is not your data or the state's guinea pig. There is no law stating that s/he must take the test. There is no program that recognizes WASL scores for admittance or placement, and if this school is utilizing them in this manner, perhaps a lawsuit will take care of that. The legislature has not certified that the WASL is appropriate for any use other than the development of an accountability system for schools. I do not trust the questions; I do not trust the scoring; and until the state decides that it is my right to view my child's scored test, I will not allow my child to take part in this secret assessment.

Juanita Doyon
Mothers Against WASL
The test stops here!
www.rereformed.com
Jedoyon@aol.com
253/846–0823

Sample Guest Column

Juanita Doyon
20421 4th Ave E
Spanaway, WA 98387
253/846–0823
June 15, 2002

Editorial Page Editor
Hometown Newspaper

Dear Mr. Editor,
Please consider the following for publication as a guest column in
your paper.

Thank you,
Juanita Doyon

Support Your Local School—Public School Parenting
in the Age of Accountability

754 words

Parents are responsible for the education and well-being of their
children. When we fully accept that responsibility, we protect our
rights and the educational rights of our children and our local
schools. Right now, there are some heavy-handed state and national
reforms being applied to our local public schools and the children
and families they serve, all in the name of "accountability." I question the wisdom of the state's intended use of the WASL (Washington Assessment of Student Learning) test scores of children to hold
administrators and teachers accountable. The plan for monetary re-
wards to schools with increased test scores would seem an invita-
tion to corruption and abuse in the administrator/teacher/student/
parent balance of power. In a climate of educational "standards," it

is most important to remember that there is no such thing as a "standard" child.

Honesty, patience, respect, and humor—staples of the parent/school relationship. School employees are people, just like parents and kids. Not every teacher deserves the "Golden Apple Award," but then, "Parent of the Year" is not a trophy I've seen on too many mantels either. The challenge is to do the best we can with what we are given to work with. This can seem a daunting task, especially in a politically driven era of educational jargon and changing curriculum. Attempting to help with third-grade math homework can cause tension headaches! Yet it is important for parents to understand third-grade math homework and sixth-grade writing projects and eighth-grade culture fair demonstrations. The more involved we are in the educational lives of our children, the better their chances of success in school and in life. Parents and schools who communicate and work together ensure the best learning opportunities for children.

Often, parents are unaware of the changes that have taken place in public schools since they were students themselves, until the first parent/teacher conference reads more like a stock report than a report card. Charts and graphs and rubrics—oh, my! If we can somehow come away still feeling like the parent, rather than the first grader, I suppose we've won the day—but do we know the score?

Most teachers do a good job of moderating assignments and curriculum to fit the students in their class and challenge them just enough to learn at their best. But parents should be the final quality control managers for schoolwork. After all, we are the closest thing to an expert on the personality and ability our own child, and our schools should respect us for this—if we approach them with reason and remember that our child isn't the only student in the school.

So what do we do if we don't understand the story problems on the growth rate of breadfruit in the Fiji Islands or the seven traits of successful writing or the multiple WASL prompts of the evening? We speak up and ask! Then, when we understand things well enough to have an opinion about them, we share that opinion, whether it agrees with the teacher or the school or the district or the state or not.

Chances are if something seems inappropriate to us as parents, it is inappropriate for our kids as students and the adults in their schools as teachers. If two-hour, nightly, second-grade homework and whining time is putting a crimp in your family *Who Wants to Be a Millionaire* and popcorn time, it is reasonable and right to let it be known you're mad as heck and you're not going to do it anymore— and neither is your child. Childhood is too short to spend crying over math problems and spelling sentences for any more than thirty minutes a night in second grade. This should be the first rule of homework in any school handbook! But it will take many reasonable, well-informed, caring parents to get it there.

WASL, COM (Certificate of Mastery), OSPI (Office of the Superintendent of Public Instruction), A+ (Academic Achievement and Accountability Commission), Legislative Education Committees—Public education in Washington State is a vast and complicated system. Our state public schools serve just over one million students. Our 296 school districts are varied in economics and diverse in population. In our state's eagerness to "improve learning" and "raise standards" the individual child is sometimes lost in the shuffle. This leaves parents and teachers to sort it all out for the good of the children in their care. Support your LOCAL school!

Juanita Doyon, Jedoyon@aol.com
WA State Coordinator for the National Assessment Reform
Network, in association with *www.Fairtest.org*
Organizer, Mothers Against WASL <*www.rereformed.com*>

Bibliography

ABE, DEBBY. 2001. "Opposition to State Tests Grows Louder; Education Officials Say Concerns About Meeting New Standards Are Misplaced." *The News Tribune.* April 22.

"ABOUT ACHIEVE BOARD OF DIRECTORS AND OFFICERS." *Achieve.org.*

BAKST, BRIAN. 2000. "Minnesota Error Latest in String of Troubles with Educational Testing." Associated Press. August 18. *nwa online.net.*

BECKER, JERRY. 2001. "CA: Testing Regulations Change." *Mathforum .org.*

BENSON, JUDY. 2002. "Giving State Tests to Students Not Fluent in English Hurts Education Group Says; Lawmakers Bring Forum to City's Edgerton School." *The Day.com.*

Bounds, Amy. 2002. "Parents Planning CSAP Boycott." *The Daily Camera.* March 9.

THE BUSINESS ROUNDTABLE. "Education and the Workforce." *brt.org*

CALA, WILLIAM, BUTTON ILLUSTRATIONS, JUANITA DOYON. 2002. "My Fight for an Alternative Diploma." *The School Administrator.* December.

CALIFORNIA DEPARTMENT OF EDUCATION. Education Code section 60640.

CLOUD, JOHN, AND JODIE MORSE. 2001. "Seceding from School Home Sweet School." *Time.com.*

COLLEGE BOARD. *Collegeboard.com.*

DENN, REBEKAH. 2002. "Initiative Backers Want to Put Politicians to Test—The WASL." *Seattle Post-Intelligencer.* May 30.

————. 2002. "Former State Education Worker Fined: Penalty for Illegally Profiting from Job Is $10,000; Her Employer Will Pay $20,000." *The Seattle Post-Intelligencer.* April 13.

EDITORIAL. 2001. "Don't Abandon the WASL Test" *The Olympian.* May 3.

THE EDUCATION TRUST. *edtrust.org.*

FESSLER, DIANA. 1997. A Report on the Work Toward National Standards, Assessments, and Certificates, Part 1. Report to the Ohio State Board of Education.

FINCHLER, JUDY. 2000. *Testing Miss Malarkey.* New York: Walker and Company.

GERSTNER, LOUIS V. JR. 2001. National Education Summit Speech. *Ibm.com.*

———. 2002. "The Tests We Know We Need." *Achieve.org.*

"THE HISTORY AND PHILOSOPHY OF RETHINKING SCHOOLS." *Rethinkingschools.org.*

HOLST, CAROL M. 2002. "ARN Resistors at Ed Department Conference in San Antonio—Improving America's Schools or Overtesting America's Kids?" *Substance.* January.

"HOMESCHOOLING." NEA 2000–2001 Resolutions B-68. *nea.org*

HOUTZ, JOLAYNE. 2000. "Temps Spend Just Minutes to Score State Education Test." *The Seattle Times.* August 27.

HUGHES, POLLY ROSS. 2002. "Teen Hopes to Restore Trust in District after Election Win." *Houston Chronicle.*

HUGHES, SHARON K. 2001. "Schools Chief Cheers Reform." *San Antonio Express-News.* December 20.

KEATING, CLARICE. 2002. "Local Residents Protest WASL Testing." *Camas-Washougal Post-Record.* March 26.

"LANDMARK EDUCATION CASE WILL HOLD STATE RESPONSIBLE FOR PERVASIVE SUBSTANDARD CONDITIONS IN PUBLIC SCHOOLS." 2002. ACLU Press Release. *Aclunc.org.*

NATIONAL CENTER FOR EDUCATION STATISTICS. 2000. *The Condition of Education.* Washington, D.C. U.S. Department of Education.

OHANIAN, SUSAN. 2001. "News from the Test Resistance Trail." *Phi Delta Kappan.* January. 363–366.

OREL, STEVE. "522 students pushed out of school in Birmingham, Alabama: 2000" Discussion with Steve. *Interversity.com.*

ORLICH, DONALD C., ROBERT J. HARDER, RICHARD C. CALLAHAN, AND HARRY W. GIBSON. 2001. *Teaching Strategies: A Guide to Better Instruction.* Boston: Houghton Mifflin Company.

PAPE, JOHN. 2002. "Letting Their Opinions Be Known Alvin: Residents Organize Weekly Forums to Speak Their Minds." *The Houston Chronicle.* January 9.

POWELL, MICHAEL. 2001. "In N.Y., Putting Down Their Pencils Parent Rebellion Against Standardized Testing Strikes at Heart of Bush Plan." *Washington Post.* May 18. A01.

"PROCLAMATION." *Sepschool.org.*

ROANE, SUSAN. 1988. *How to Work a Room.* New York: Warner Books.

ROBERTS, GREGORY. 2002. "If Raises Go, So Should WASL, Union Argues." *Seattle Post-Intelligencer.* February 21.

ROSS, J.J., AND NANCE CONFER. "Introduction." *ParentDirectedEducation.org.*

SCARSDALE SCHOOL BOARD. 2002. "Statement on Testing and Assessment."

BOARD OF EDUCATION MEETING. February 11. *scarsdaleschools.k12 .ny.us*

SHAW, LINDA. 2001. "Teachers become WASL insiders: State sending 175 to help grade tests." *The Seattle Times.* May 3.

STOVER, JOANN. 1960. *If Everybody Did.* New York: David McKay Company, Inc.

TOPPO, GREG. 2002. "Vermont Governor Opposed to Education Plan." Associated Press. April 18.

U.S. DEPARTMENT OF EDUCATION. 1983. *A Nation at Risk: The Imperative for Educational Reform. Ed.gov/pubs/NatAtRisk/*

U.S. DEPARTMENT OF EDUCATION. 1998. *Goals 2000: Reforming Education to Improve Student Achievement. Ed.gov/pubs/ G2KReforming/*

U.S. DEPARTMENT OF EDUCATION. 2001. *The Elementary and Secondary Education Act (The No Child Left Behind Act of 2001). ed.gov/ legislation/ESEA02/*